# CLICHÉS
# AND
# COMMON SENSE

# CLICHÉS
# AND
# COMMON SENSE

## Amos Moses Terry

E-BookTime, LLC
Montgomery, Alabama

# Clichés And Common Sense

Library of Congress Control Number: 2005929917

ISBN: 1-59824-043-9 Hardcover
ISBN: 1-59824-044-7 Trade Paperback
ISBN: 1-59824-045-5 Adobe E-book

Published August 2005
E-BookTime, LLC
6598 Pumpkin Road
Montgomery, AL 36108
www.e-booktime.com

# DEDICATION

My son, Philip, was a special person. His only fault was: He was a "Carolina Gamecock". His dad (me) was, and is, a "Fighting Tiger" mortal, knock-down, drag-out enemies. (And there would not be any doubt in anyone's mind!)

I remember, one time, when he gave me a Christmas present: A picture of a tiger on a mirror with a gamecock rooster on his back with a whip in his claws. The rooster was riding on the tiger's back and whipping him. I gave the picture back, and my son hung it on a wall in his bedroom.

We attended several Carolina/Clemson football games together. Philip would jump up and down and holler, when Carolina made a good play, and I would do the same, when Clemson returned the favor. People would look at us with question marks in their eyes.

Philip was smart. He inherited that from me. He did not learn it at Carolina (just in case you Carolina fans need to know).

He was a walking encyclopedia and very witty. He was always making people laugh. He was the life of any party.

I miss him (Lord, I miss him!) If you have ever lost a child, you know what I'm talking about. He was in the prime of his life when the Lord called him home. Philip Bootsie (that's a nickname that I gave him when he was a baby), we all miss you so much. But we will see you on the other side. Until then, I dedicate this book in your memory, my son.

# CONTENTS

# CONTENTS

# CONTENTS

# ACKNOWLEDGMENTS

I'm glad I'm an American. I'm glad I'm a Southern born American. I'm glad that I'm a country boy American.

My heritage is what this book is all about. It's my life stories, adventures, experiences, and reflections. I could not begin to list all the folks who contributed. But, you can be sure that they were mostly Southerners, like me.

I do want to thank a few people though: My wife, Imogene and my step daughter, Debbie who know how to work the computer much better than I, and Steven Jackson, a fine young fellow, who helped me to get the sketches on a disc. They are people who talk with a Southern drawl and use clichés.

Simple folks are the best kind (I think). But simple doesn't mean that they are not smart. There are some wise old geezers who are simple, everyday, shop-worn folks. We have many of them down South.

Just because some folks speak with a drawl, just because they may use a lot of clichés, just because they don't use a lot of big dictionary words doesn't mean that they are not smart.

What is wisdom, anyway? Is it book knowledge? Is it having a mind so complicated that no one can understand what you are saying? Is that wisdom? Shucks no! That's not wisdom.

Wisdom is having simple answers to complicated problems.

Wisdom is: "Why haven't I thought of that"!

Wisdom is: "Plain as the nose on your face"!

Wisdom is: "You reap what you sow"!

Wisdom is: "All work and no play makes Jack a dull boy"! (Paw should have been told this one)!

Wisdom is: "Beauty is skin deep"!

Wisdom is: "Love covers a multitude of sins"!

Wisdom is: "Use it or lose it"!

Wisdom is: "You can teach an old dog new tricks"!

You can probably add more clichés to the list maybe better than these, especially, if you are an old time Southerner.

Jesus taught in parables that were simple, parables about everyday life that simple folks could understand. The complicated minds of that day could not understand Jesus.

They were looking for a Messiah who would be riding on a white horse, in shining armor, who would lead them into battle and conquer all their foes with military might. But a simple Messiah came. They could not understand.

Life doesn't get any less simple than that of our Lord. Born to a lowly peasant girl. Born in a stable. The first to know that He had come were lowly shepherds, farmers but wise men. That, my friends, is wisdom!

Jesus taught in parables. Southerners, in times past, talked with drawls and used many clichés. Southerners get to the point fast. They don't use a lot of unnecessary words, and clichés were a simple way of getting their points across.

I am, in no way, trying to compare Southerners with Jesus. I'm not that stupid. I'm just trying to explain the similarity of clichés and parables. Simple minds can understand parables and simple minds can get the gist of clichés.

Folks, down South, in years gone by, were simple, down to earth farmers. They used many clichés. I think most of the clichés used in this book originated back then. And, in my opinion, to fully understand and appreciate clichés, like Jesus' parables, you must be a down to earth, every day, simple person.

Life was certainly different down South in the old days than it is today. There aren't many cotton fields, mules and wagons, and simple farmers left anymore.

We are losing our Southern drawl, fast. We are losing our neighbors, too. (They haven't moved. It's just that we don't visit as much anymore).

Life is more complicated. We don't enjoy simple pleasures as much as we did in the old days. Pretty soon, we may not even enjoy using old Southern clichés anymore (heavens forbid!)

I hope that this book may help bring back some pleasant memories. And, if you happen to be a young person of Southern heritage, that you will get the gist of how life was in the old South and that you will be proud to say: "I'm from Dixie Land. A way down South in Dixie!

I hope you have a nice day.

Amos Moses Terry

# CLICHÉ NO. 1

## PEOPLE WHO LIVE IN GLASS HOUSES SHOULD NOT THROW ROCKS

It's alright for people who live in the shanty villages of India to throw rocks, and to play flutes, too, to keep the slithering Cobra snakes from sneaking in and spitting poisonous venom into their eyes. That's alright!

There are many old Indian men, sitting around on their haunches, selling newspapers in Calcutta, that have a cloudy eye that they can't see out of because of a Cobra snake spitting venom into their eyes (Oh! If they only had thrown a rock at those snakes!)

Snakes are like old Satan, evil creatures. They sneak up on their prey without making a sound. They hide in the grass and leaves, camouflaged to look like their surroundings (The same way Satan camouflages himself to blend in with the crowd) and then, when some innocent, happy-go-lucky, rabbit, or bird, or mouse, (or naïve young person) comes hop-hop-hopping along ("bingo"!) The snake, or Satan, strikes with poisonous venom that leaves the victim blinded, paralyzed, and helpless!

15

It's alright to throw rocks at snakes and Old Satan!

It's alright, too, for boys, especially country boys who live out in the sticks, to throw rocks at tin cans, birds, grass hoppers, squirrels' nests, and at knot holes in hollow trees. That kind of rock throwing is alright. It's alright, too, for boys to use sling shots on such things.

If you are a boy, especially if you are a country boy and don't learn to throw rocks, you stand a chance of not developing into a well rounded, masculine man (In other words: you might become a sissy, or a weasel, or a dude, or a nerd).

Boys ought to learn to throw rocks, climb trees, skin their knees, and get dirty! That's part of being a boy. (Of course, I might be prejudiced because I had such a boyhood. But, I'm pretty sure that I'm right about it).

I'll tell you this: "I can walk into a room filled with men and I can pick out the men who have thrown rocks when they were boys. They are masculine, confident, happy, and virile!" Look at their hands. That's how you can tell.

Look at Jimmy Carters hands: piano hands! Look at Bill Clinton's hands: saxophone hands! Look at "Abe" Lincoln's hands and Ronald Reagan's hands: hands that have wielded an axe, and, yes, thrown rocks at varmints! Do you see what I mean?

It's alright, too, for Palestinian refugees, who live in the mud hut camps, to throw rocks at Israelis' tanks, helicopters, and armored vehicles (I wonder where all those rocks in Palestine came from? They seem never to run out of rocks).

Anyway, it's alright for the Palestinians to throw rocks at the Israelis for the rocks couldn't make a dent in the armored vehicles anyway. And, if the Israelis happen to turn their big guns in the direction of the rock throwing Palestinians and blast them to Kingdom Come, that's alright, too, for the Palestinians would be immediately martyred into the presence of Allah who would give each of them ten beautiful, gorgeous virgins for all of eternity. Hey! That's alright!

But what about the ten virgins? What do they get? They get to share the dirty, unshaved, reeking warriors for that's all that the virgins deserve. They are women and women don't count in

Allah's Kingdom! Huh? Yeah. That's what they say. Ain't it a shame?

But...But people who live in glass houses should not throw rocks. First of all: They wouldn't know how. The glass houses that I'm talking about are "sky scrappers" (You've seen'em). They are in big cities.

Everyone knows that "city slickers" don't know how to throw rocks. They don't have any rocks to throw. The streets are paved, and not like the dirt roads that country boys live on. And even if the "city slickers" could find a rock, they couldn't throw it very far because: They are "sissies", "clumsies", "Casanovas" with "piano hands". They couldn't hit the side of a barn with a rock.

People who live in glass houses should not throw rocks. They should not get into a rock battle with country boys. They should not be like some of those foreign gorillas that shoot at our soldiers from "Holy" places and think that our soldiers can't shoot back!

Country boys would care less about destroying glass houses or "Holy" places, if such places were used by the enemy to fire at them.

Country boys know how to use axes, hoes, shovels, guns, and rocks. They are masculine, virile, confident, and decisive. Don't mess with them period, unless you are ready to be blasted into the presence of Allah.

People who live in glass houses should not throw rocks!

# CLICHÉ NO. 2

## RED AS A BEET

Do you like beets? Not all people like beets. In fact, not many city people like beets. But I like'em. I guess that's the country in me. I like beets with cabbage. I like beets with boiled potatoes with white gravy. I like beets with corn bread and white-soupy butter beans. If you don't like such things, you are not "Down South" country.

Down south, you will find beets planted in most every farmer's garden because we like beets.

However, sometimes, when I'm not around other southern country folks, I'm a bit ashamed to admit that I eat beets. For instance: When I was a G.I. soldier, over in Germany, a long, long ways from home, away from my dear beloved South, I saw German farmers hauling wagon loads of beets to feed to their Animals (I couldn't believe it!) They grew beets to feed their big "ole" bobbed tail horses; their big "ole" fat brown cows; their big "ole" dirty wooly sheep. These animals were like me: They ate beets and liked'em!

18

But, because I saw the Germans feeding beets to animals, I was a bit ashamed to tell my buddies from the north that we served beets on our dinner tables in the south. I was, also, ashamed to tell them what else we ate down south: pork bellies with grits; opossums with candid yams; turnip greens with cornbread and buttermilk, etc.

But, I bet, if the truth was known, that those Germans ate beets, too-especially the German farm gals. They had red cheeks like a beet and they were big and fat like those brown cows.

I'm pretty sure that those German farm gals ate beets and maybe a lot of other stuff that we southern farm boys ate. It took a lot of energy for those German girls to do their farm chores. Like: shoveling manure (horse, cow, and sheep. I've seen'em) on the fields of beets in the springtime.

I don't know if we southern country folks, and maybe the German girls, are the only ones to eat beets or not, but I feel that maybe the British do, also. They got those rosy cheeks from something. If it wasn't from eating beets, what was it? It could have been from eating kidney pies. Kidneys are red, too, and the British eat lots of them. If I was a British, limey soldier boy, I would be ashamed to tell all that we eat. Wouldn't you?

The German farm girls and the British blokes are not the only ones with rosy cheeks (red like a beet). The Irish have red cheeks, too. But, I think, their red cheeks came from drinking that mean "ole" Irish whiskey. Irish whiskey is almost as mean as "white lightning" the kind that "paw" used to drink.

The Irish are like a lot of "Down South" southerners: They like to party (Of course many southerners are Irish, too). I'm part Irish, part Scott, and part "Lord knows what else". (Well, the USA is known as the "melting pot"). I'm an example. I'm blended, like blended whiskey.

But Irish whiskey has not been blended. It comes straight. And the Irish drink barrels of it. They love it. It sets their bellies on fire, until they seem that they will explode and many do! Their tempers flare. Their noses get red and their cheeks, too, like a beet. Do not mess with an Irishman with rosy cheeks, unless you are ready to be blasted into "Kingdom Come".

Eating lots of beets, kidney pies, and drinking Irish whiskey might cause one to have red cheeks, but there is something else that might cause them to be red: Mountain oysters! Have you tried them? Me neither. But, I bet, that they could cause red cheeks. I know they would me, if anyone ever caught me eating them. I would be so embarrassed!

And another thing: All red cheeks are not caused by eating and drinking. Some are caused by standing too close to the fire!

In the old days, down south, farmers lived in ramshackle, creaky old houses that had cracks in the floor, high off the ground, on rock pillars. In the winter, winds would howl under the house and would, sometimes, lift the linoleum off the floor. Linoleum was what most farm houses had for floor covering.

If you wanted to stay warm, you had to almost get in the fire. That's what a lot of farm girls tried to do. They would back up to the fire and lift their dresses to warm their hind ends. Often, they would get too close to the fire and they would burn those cheeks! Yeah, I know what you are thinking, but they didn't wear any. Bloomers, that is!

# CLICHÉ NO. 3

## THE GRASS IS GREENER ON THE OTHER SIDE OF THE FENCE

Cows like to eat grass. That's what they eat most of the time. But they will eat other stuff, too, if it is on the other side of the fence! They will stand in knee high, plush, green grass pastures and, yet, stick their heads under the fence to take a swipe, with their long tongues, at nothing but dry rag weeds that are on the other side of the fence. I have seen it happen, more than once. Cows had rather eat weeds on the other side of the fence than to eat delicious, tasty, fertilized, green grass in their own pastures!

And do you know what? People are often like those cows, especially women shoppers. They will stand at the locked doors of large department stores: Maceys, Richs, Belks, Pennys, etc., etc. on super sales days, and threaten to knock the doors down if they are not opened immediately! And the moment the doors are unlocked, the women will stampede, like a herd of wild buffaloes, down the aisles to racks of clothes and to display tables with items marked: "ON SALE' with red tags.

It doesn't matter if there are similar items, or nicer, elsewhere in the store that are cheaper, but are not marked "On Sale" with red tags. There is something about red tags that makes women's hormones flow. They go after those red tag items like a fighting bull goes after the matador's red flag!

Department stores have learned about women's attraction to the red flag sales. So, once a year, or twice, or three times, or four, or every two weeks, stores will have a sale. They jack up the prices, get out the red tags, and put them on "hard to sale" items. Then they advertise like mad, with colorful inserts in local newspapers that show nice, trim, beautiful young women clad in tight fitting garments and wait for the stampede (And the stores will keep the doors locked until the exact second that the sale is advertised to begin).

Excitement? Yes! Women like competition. They like to race other women, like in the Olympics, to see if they can beat them to the bargains (huh?) marked with red tags.

But listen! Women's shopping for "red tag specials" is "not a drop in the bucket" compared to some men. You've heard about them: Those that lust for the grass (pretty ladies) that seems greener on the other side of the fence (in other words: in "no man's land").

Look what happened to the well- known TV evangelist (or two, or three, or "umpteen" evangelists). The grass seemed greener on the other side of the fence for them.

Even though the evangelist had a beautiful wife (beauty is in the eyes of the beholder), with long, false, glittering, eyelashes that flashed sparks when she blinked, and dressed "fit to kill" in a sparkling, tight fitting gown, with a carefully sprayed "up swept" hair-do with dangling curls (or was it a wig? I couldn't tell), and with a sweet, enticing, accented feminine voice, somewhat like Zaa-Zaa's. That's what the evangelist had awaiting him at home! (And I forgot to mention that he had an empire the size of Manhattan). But it all came crumbling down when he took a chance with a beautiful young girl that was in "no man's land" on the other side of the fence!

22

And another man: An executive, an executive in the highest office in the land, "The Oval Office"! (How stupid can one get?). The "red tag specials" for the ladies did not compare to the lust that this man had for a young girl and the man had a beautiful wife (beauty is in the eyes of the beholder), an eloquent wife, an important public figure (yes), awaiting him at home when he got off work.

Why does the grass always, ever and always, seem greener on the other side of the fence? Why can't we all be satisfied with the good things of life that the Lord has given us? I'll tell you why: "We are greedy, carnal, human beings, with big physical appetites.

We lust for the forbidden fruits, things that will destroy our spiritual souls, material things, things that give us sensual pleasures in the heat of the moment but will destroy our souls for all of eternity!

If we would only stop and take a moment to think about the consequences, the grass on the other side of the fence would not seem quite so green!

# CLICHÉ NO. 4

## IF YOU LAY DOWN WITH DOGS, YOU WILL GET UP WITH FLEAS

I used to have a Rottweiler dog. His name was Bert. He was a good dog. He was a smart dog. He was a beautiful dog; but he had fleas! I know he had fleas because he was always scratching himself with his hind paws.

Now, if I had given "ole" Bert a bath, once a week, or twice, with strong lye soap, or with some other strong, flea killing soap, I might have gotten rid of the fleas which caused him so much misery. But I didn't do that.

I didn't bathe Bert because, I guess, I'm lazy. I didn't bathe him because I wouldn't like for him to sling soapy water all over me when I wet him down. I didn't bathe him because I don't like to smell a wet dog.

Poor ole Bert, he would just have to suffer with his fleas.

I don't know where he got the fleas. We didn't have any other dogs. But my wife did have a cat that would rub up against Bert back and forth, like cats will do. I guess, maybe, the cat might have given Bert the fleas, she had'em, too. I didn't bathe the cat either because I don't like cats. My wife does; but I don't.

Now, I have always heard that if you lay down with dogs, you will get up with fleas.

Bert had not been lying down with dogs, as far as I know. So, I guess, the cat must have given Bert the fleas. But he, also, might have gotten them from somewhere else (Like from people who live up the road, in a trailer, who have several shaggy headed little boys).

I'm speaking from experience. I was a boy once, a long time ago, and I was shaggy headed. My hair was blond (almost white. My sisters called me "grandpa"). It seemed that I always needed a haircut. Well, I got lice in that beautiful, long, shaggy, blond hair. And I would scratch, like ole Bert scratching his fleas.

I don't know how I got those lice; but I suspect it was from my cotton mill neighborhood buddies. They had'em also. You catch lice the same way that a dog catches fleas, from those you hang out with.

I can see my cotton mill buddies mamas, now, scrubbing their heads, with lice killing soap, on the back porches of their cotton mill hill houses. Their mamas thought that I had given them the lice. I could tell by the way they looked at me. And maybe I did. What a shame!

But my mama didn't scrub my head to get rid of the lice. She had "paw" give me a haircut, with hand clippers, out in the back yard. He cut off all my beautiful blond hair. He skinned me! I was as bald as a turnip. I hated to go to school. Everyone would know why I was bald: Lice! How shameful to have lice and everyone know it!

But you could see a lot of bald headed boys at my school back in those days. They had lice, too. And their "paws" had given them a haircut, like mine, too.

That was a common remedy, in those days, for lice.

Lice spread from people to people. Fleas spread from dog to dog. If you lay down with people who have lice, you will get up with lice. If you lay down with dogs that have fleas, you will get up with fleas (And that might not be all that you will get: Crabs, scabies, seven year itch and maybe some other things).

I better stop talking about this. I'm starting to itch all over!

# CLICHÉ NO. 5

## WHEN HELL FREEZES OVER

Life, in the old days down south, was quite different from that of today. People were not in a big hurry like they are today. Days seemed longer. People worked harder. There were not nearly as many fat people.

Back then, every family had a garden, a milk cow, some chickens, and a pig, and maybe some goats. Life moved at a much slower pace.

Then, along came Henry Ford. He changed everything. He invented the assembly line for producing cars. The pace of life picked up. As cars began to go faster and faster, life began to move faster and faster.

Back then, most families, not all but most, were earning enough to buy one of Henry Ford's model "T". The model "T" was not much more than a rubber tired wagon with a gas engine.

This vehicle was suited for the muddy roads down south. The axles were high off the ground and the narrow tires could stay in the ruts better.

At first, most families used their cars only on weekends to go to town, or to church, or to visit their country friends and family kin. But, as life went on, more and more people bought the cars. Cars became a common sight around the neighborhoods and on the roads. Horses and mules got used to seeing, and hearing, the cars and farmers had less trouble keeping the animals in check when meeting the vehicles on a country lane.

With the advent of cars, life in the rural south began to change. People didn't have nearly as much time for the little things that make life enjoyable, like sitting on their front porches and chitt-chatting with neighbors until it was time to blow out the lamps and go to bed. Like hanging around livery stables on Saturday afternoons and enjoying the "wheeling and dealing" in trading of farm animals, or like walking down town, the whole gangs, moms and dads and the many children (families were big) to a community tent revival, where the offering plates consisted of several foot tubs and with a challenge from the country preacher: "If you want a blessing from God, you will fill the tubs up with folding money"; or like going to a textile league baseball game, just about everyone did in the community, and joining in the fun of heckling the umpires. That was fun!

Yes, I think, the mass production of cars changed the way of life, not only for the south, but also for the whole world. People, the world over, began to travel to here to there and to nowhere in particular, just get out and go. When you are on the go so much, little things that amount to so much are neglected and fall by the wayside.

After starting the mass production of cars, the world started to mass produce everything. Buy and sell and get gain. Money! Money! Money!

That's what has ruined the south and the whole world. And changed the pace of life.

The emphasis of life is money! Money buys everything you need! That, my friends, is a lie! Satan, himself, concocted this lie. Satan has deceived the world. And the whole world has swallowed this lie "hook line and sinker".

Now, every good fisherman knows that when a fish swallows the hook, the line and the sinker that you got'em. And Satan has the whole world on a string.

The south and all of America is not what it used to be. Money has ruined us. We are, no longer, just plain, honest, good "ole", hard working, country folks. We are (most of us) after that "all mighty dollar"!

I'm sorry. But that's the way it is folks. The dollar is destroying our souls (dope peddlers, Hollywood, the entertainment community, politicians, and the computer internet are destroying our souls).

Satan must be jumping up and down with glee. He has us where he wants us. We are dumb, dumb, and dumb! (Not just the blonds; But we all are).

And hell will freeze over before we wake up and come to our senses and change our ways and start loving our neighbors and loving God again.

# CLICHÉ NO. 6

## THE POT SHOULD NOT CALL THE KETTLE BLACK

People, in times gone by, used to do their cooking over open fires (I've seen it in history books about the Pilgrims, frontiersmen, cowboys, etc.)

Most of their cooking was done in cast iron vessels: pots, frying pans, and kettles. My mama used to have one of those cast iron pots. She didn't use it to cook over an open flame (I'm not quite that old); but she did use it to cook on a wood burning stove. That's how old I am, and that's old enough! Just how old, I'm not saying. I will say this, however: "I can no longer cut the mustard". Now, you know, that's pretty old. So let's just leave it at that!

Anyway, in order to cook with cast iron vessels, the fire must be pretty hot. Any "old Time" mama, who has done much cooking, can tell you that if you are gonna get dinner ready by dinner time, twelve noon sharp, in time for the hungry "cow punchers", "plow hands", and "lumberjacks" to sit down and eat and get back to work the flames must shoot up and lick the cast iron pots, frying pans and kettles from all sides.

But, before the fire gets hot enough to make the lids on the vessels jump up and down, there is a lot of black, bellowing smoke. In time, this black, inky black, smoke turns the cast iron cooking vessels black: The pots, the kettles and the frying pans. But, cooking with the black cast iron vessels is what makes the vittles good!

Green pole beans, with whole red Irish potatoes, cooked on a smoky fire, in a cast iron pot, are good! They taste better than beans and potatoes cooked in Paul Revere copper plated stainless steel cookware on an electric stove. And tea, boiled in black cast iron kettles over an open fire, tastes better than tea made with modern tea bags. And eggs, and ham, and grits are yummy, yummy when cooked in a cast iron frying pan out on the range ask any "old cowhand"!

Pots get black. Pans and kettles get black. And the blacker they get, the better the food tastes.

America is the "melting pot". We have people of all nationalities, white, yellow, tan and black.

We should not use racial slurs and call our brothers: "you white jerk", or "you Chinese hippie", or "you black son of a you know what". We should not do that! It's not polite. We are all in this together. If we use slurs, we are hurting ourselves for we are family. All of us are Americans. If we slur one another, it's like the pot calling the kettle black.

Now, if one of the same race wants to use such remarks, that's ok. For instance: I had two black American brick masons doing some work for me. Some black girls came by and started kidding with the masons and interfering with their work. When the girls left, one of the black masons said, and I quote: "They better keep their black asses away from here"! Is that ok? I think it is. But it may be like the pot calling the kettle black!

# CLICHÉ NO. 7

## OUT OF THE FIRE INTO THE FRYING PAN

I know that this is a "Down South", old-timer's saying. It's old time for it had to have originated way back yonder when fires were the sources of heat for cooking. It had to be before electric stoves, microwaves, hot plates, etc.. I know, also, that the saying is from down south because "Down South" southerners use frying pans more than anybody.

We fry chicken, southern style, like nobody else. We fry chittlins (to use in our corn pone), southern style, like nobody else. We fry "poke" chops, southern style in white milk gravy, like nobody else.

If you don't like fried things to eat, you better not come down to the good ole South for that's what you will get. Frying is what southern cooking is all about!

Everything gets fried down south (chickens, pigs, fish, turtles, 'possums and even turkeys). Have you tried fried turkey? They are yummy, yummy.

Pretty soon, I guess, we will start frying vegetables: green tomatoes, okra, yams, cabbage, and a lot of other stuff. (Oh! I beg your pardon. My wife says that we already are frying these things). You can tell that I am not much of a cook. I just eat it when it's put on the table, southern style, with my head bent low, and with my elbows on the table. I know that is not good manners to eat like that but I got in that habit when I was young. I came from a large family and if you were not prepared to eat when mama put it on the table, you might get left out.

Meat and vegetables are not the only things to get fried down south. We fry people. At least, we use to.

Georgia used to have an electric chair in the Georgia State Penitentiary in Reidsville. They used it to fry criminals: murderers, rapists, traitors, etc. I saw the chair, once when I was a Gideon handing out Bibles to the inmates in the prison. A guard escorted me to the floor with cells on "death row" (Gosh I would have hated to be in one of those cells waiting for my name to be called). And there it was: "The Frying Machine"! The "All Electric Chair"!

It looked ages old, like an antique, worn from its many uses. I saw the switch. It was a big high voltage switch with a long handle that some designated deputy or warden had to throw to send an electric current rushing through the brain, the arms, wrists, body, and legs of the condemned inmates.

The guard told me how they prepared the inmates for the "Hot Seat": They shaved their heads, wrists, and ankles and put a conductive grease substance on these areas. Then, they put a metal helmet, metal wrist and ankle bands on the inmate. The helmet was connected to a high voltage cable. The wrist and ankle bands were connected to a ground conductor. Thus, when that big switch was thrown, the high voltage current would rush through the victim's brain, down through the wrists and ankles to ground (Talking about frying). The inmate would jerk two or three times and that was it! That was all she wrote! There would be no more crimes from this victim of Georgia's frying pan!

When the guard described the picture to me, I could visualize the scene with the criminals dying in that chair. That penitentiary

33

gave me the creeps! It was eerie! I could feel evil spirits in that place!

The guard told me the story about one inmate that was electrocuted in that chair: He was an important figurehead in a Georgia county (like Boss Hog in The Dukes of Hazard). He had the county government under his control. But he did not control a local sheriff.

That sheriff was relentless in his pursuit of a killer that had killed a dirt poor farm hand. And the sheriff got his man (that big boss man of the county)!

The poor, penniless, farm hand was murdered for stealing a cow. Actually, I think, the cow belonged to the poor man but he used the cow as collateral and had borrowed money from the county boss man.

The killer burned the poor man's body on a big pine log fire and threw the man's ashes into a creek. But the sheriff was able to gather some of the ashes that had caught on some trash in the creek, prove they were human ashes, convince a terrified, scared to death, colored farm hand, that had been ordered to burn the body, to testify in court, and the sheriff got a conviction of the big county figurehead.

Someone wrote a book about it: "Murder In Coweta County". If you are interested, you should get the book and read it. The book will give you all the details. Hollywood, also, made a movie about the murder. I think Andy Griffith and Johnny Cash starred in the movie.

Anyway, the prison guard at the Georgia State penitentiary told me how this murderer met his fate: It took three or four deputies to bring this big man from his cell, set him down in the electric chair, and strap him in. All the time, he was cussing, screaming, kicking, and slinging the deputies. After he was strapped into the chair, he was still cussing and fuming, and using God's name in vain when the switch was thrown and he left this world! All I can say is: "What a way to go"!

Out of the fire (the pine log bon fire ashes) into the frying pan (Georgia's Electric Chair)!! Wow!

# CLICHÉ NO. 8

## PRACTICE MAKES PERFECT

NOTE:
SHE NEVER MADE IT TO CARNEGIE HALL EVEN THOUGH SHE PRACTICED, PRACTICED, PRACTICED!

MY DAUGHTER, JANE

When I was a boy, many, many years ago, but I still remember, I could throw a baseball, I believe, ninety miles per hour, like the big leagues. And I could hit the target, too. I'm not bragging. But I didn't get to practice much.

I didn't get to play baseball because "paw" kept me busy. He kept me busy hoeing cotton, pulling corn, plowing a mule, etc. (Busy with farming chores).

But, I bet, if "paw" had known and fully understood that my talent was throwing a baseball and not farming (which I hated) that he would have excused me and allowed me to go practice baseball, especially, if "paw" had realized just how much money professional ballplayers got.

If I had been allowed to practice, there ain't no telling how good I would have gotten. I might have become famous like Dizzy Dean", or "Spit Baller" Gaylord Perry, Or "Knuckle Baller" Phil Nickro. I know I sound like I'm dreaming, but I believe that it's possible that I could have become "Famous Amos" the Fire Baller.

Oh! If "paw" had only allowed me to practice, I might have made enough money to allow him to lay by his cotton forever, sell his mules, get in his dilapidated Model "A" Ford touring car, the one without the top, and go fishing everyday in the Savannah river, instead of just going occasionally with his fish baskets.

Practice is what it takes. But I didn't realize it when I was a boy and "paw" didn't realize it either. I know better, now. But it is too late (Much, much too late).

I have finally come to my senses. It's too late for me, but it's not too late for my grandson, Hunter. Hunter has inherited my talent. His father thinks it's his talent that Hunter inherited. His father was a big leaguer, but Hunter has my talent.

That's the reason I send him to Jack Legett's Clemson baseball camp. I pay Hunter's expenses. I told Coach Legett to teach Hunter how to pitch, how to throw sliders, curves, knuckle balls, etc., and that if Hunter ever got good enough to play on Clemson's baseball team that I would give the coach a big kiss on each cheek. Poor Hunter! He will probably have to work twice as hard to make Clemson's team!

I expect great things from my grandson. I have set high goals for him. I want him to achieve the things that I could not achieve. I expect him to make lots of money and pay me back (with interest) That I might take a vacation and go basking in the sun on the Rivera, that I might see Rome, the Grand Canyon, Niagara Falls, and other exotic places, and that I might live the life of Riley (for at least a season) before I die.

But, it will take practice, practice, and practice for Hunter. I think that he realizes this for he is a real hustler!

Many boys, and girls, don't fully develop their potentials while they are young, and before they know it they are old, like me. And, when they do finally wake up, they will discover that it is too late.

Opportunities abound everywhere. If one is on his toes and has ambition, he can make the big time! But, if one is to get to the top, he must preserver. He must work, work, and work. He must practice, practice, and practice. Practice makes perfect.

There was a tourist in New York City. He was lost and trying to find his way to Carnegie Hall. He saw a hippie looking fellow, with long hair, shabby clothes, earrings, nose rings, etc. standing at the street corner. The man went up to the hippie and said: "Hey fellow, I wonder if you can tell me how to get to Carnegie Hall?" The hippie replied: "Yeah man! Practice, Practice, Practice!"

# CLICHÉ NO. 9

## THERE'S GOING TO BE HELL TO PAY

I know that I'm going to get a lot of arguments from my Christian friends, but I believe in evolution. There's no question in my mind. But, listen: I also believe that there is a living God. God is in control. God is the creator of all things.

I believe that God created man after His own likeness, in His own image. Therefore, man is a living soul. Man is a spiritual being that will live forever, somewhere: heaven or hell. That's what I believe.

Now, just how God went about creating man and the time, I don't think anyone knows for sure. I differ with the theologians and with the atheists. I believe that God used the evolution process to create His ultimate creation: "Man"! I'm not going to give you all the reasons why I believe this (I don't have enough paper). But, I also believe, that even though it was God's plan to form man through the evolution process, that there was an appointed time that God breathed the breath of life into man and he became a living, spiritual soul. God is a spirit and He communicates with The Holy spirit with man. He has spoken to all people, everywhere. Therefore, no one has an excuse for not believing in Him!

But, there was definitely a time when man lived in caves. There was a time when men were not much more than animals. Before this, we don't have much evidence about how men lived. They had crude weapons: Stone axes, stone arrows, and spears, etc. We know this. I have found stone arrowheads and stone tommy hawks on my land.

At one time, a long time ago, more than 6000 years that some theologians teach, man existed on the earth and he was definitely more like an animal than he was a civilized human being, his lifestyle; his communications; his method of travel; his manners; his morals, etc. were not much better than the animals.

He depended on food from the land: Animals, berries, birds, fish, fruits, nuts, etc. We know this because of the evidence we have found in caves and camp sites of early man.

As the evolution progressed, man became more intelligent. He learned through his mistakes. This, my friends, is evolution. He became wiser. He began to explore outside his small domain and began to experiment and to discover new things, like fire; electricity; petroleum, etc.

Man's communication, at first, was with grunts, and motions, and sign language. But, as he became more intelligent, he began to make sounds and to form words and to communicate verbally with his fellow man.

He began to learn that two heads are better than just one (though some people still think they know it all), and he began to band together with other humans to form clans and armies.

He moved out of the caves and began to build shelters. He became more sociable, more rational, saner, and less and less like his relatives, the animals. But man was, and still is until this day, a mixture of a spiritual being, inherited from his spiritual father, God, and animal being, inherited from his animal ancestor. Disagree if you want, but that is the conclusion that I have reached in my finite mind.

God has spoken. God has revealed Himself to me. And He has revealed Himself to all people: Asians; Africans; Indians; Italians;

Spaniards; Americans (All people). If you go to the most primitive tribes, to those that still live almost like animals, in the jungles, God has been there. He has spoken to them.

All men have a choice: Feed our spiritual nature and try to live as God leads us, or ignore our spiritual nature and feed the animal within us: Our lusts; greed; physical appetites; sensual pleasures, and live like animals.

Yes, man has a choice to make, and the vast majority have made the wrong choice!

Instead of man's spiritual nature taking root and growing and flourishing and dominating, as God desired, Man's spiritual nature became emaciated and began to dry up and to die. His animal nature of lusts, anger, lies, immorality, and unruliness grew and abounded.

God was grieved! This grieved our Holy and Righteous and Spiritual God. This grieved God so much that He decided to start the evolution process all over again, with one man and his family who were more spiritual than all the others. This man was Noah.

I believe that! I believe that God became so displeased with man that He sent a big, gigantic flood that covered the whole world. There's evidence of this, at least in my finite mind. How did the sands of the Sahara Desert get there? How did the Grande Canyon form? How did the seashells become deposited in Oklahoma? How did oil, fossil fuel, evolve in such unpredictable places like: Alaska, Siberia, the deserts, off shore in the oceans, etc? The only answer that satisfies this old inquisitive mind is: There was a calamity like this world has never seen before! (Like: torrents of rain coming down for forty days and nights all over the world)! The weight of this water caused the axis of the earth to shift. Animals and vegetation died. Rushing mighty rivers formed. Icebergs broke loose and plowed over lands making plains and valleys, and Grande Canyons. The sun came up and went down in a different place.

Yes, I believe that there was a calamity. God showed his anger with man, and He started over with Noah and his family.

But listen: Man was still a stubborn beast. So God planned: "I will send My Son to them to teach them My Ways."

God so loved the world that He sent His only Begotten Son that who so ever believeth on him should not perish, but have everlasting life.

That was God's final plan for man!

So Jesus, The Son of God, came. He was born to a virgin, in the flesh (both God and man) and He walked upon the face of this earth preaching a message that had never been heard before: "Love God. Love your neighbors. Love your enemies. Forgive those who trespass against you. Come unto me and I will give you rest. Open the door of your heart and I will come in and abide with you forever! I will help you to overcome those animal temptations. Follow me and I will lead you to the Promised Land!

What do you think? Do you think man is listening? Do you think man is evolving into a better spiritual being? Not me!

I think man is still letting his animal nature dominate. Look around. Look at the terrorists! Look at Hollywood! Look at the entertainment community! Aren't they exploiting the animal nature of man?

Yes, I believe in evolution. I believe that God intended for man to evolve to be like Jesus: Love, kindness, meekness, giving, forgiving, mercy, compassion, etc.

I believe that God is very, very disappointed in man whom He created to have fellowship with Him.

Man has a free will and a free choice. But man has made the wrong choice.

He is still, until this day, feeding his animal nature more than he feeds his spiritual nature. He is not evolving according to God's plan. He is not accepting God's only Begotten Son to be his Lord.

I believe that one day, very soon, God is going to say: "Enough is enough. I've had it up to here with man (stubborn beasts)", and God is going to call His Saints home. Lord I want to be in that number. Don't you? And God is going to destroy this old rotten world with fire! And then, He is going to create a new heaven and a new earth, where there will be no more of this fusing, and shooting, and lying, and stealing, and living like animals!

Evolution? Yes, I believe in it. But. But. But. There is a day coming when there is going to be hell to pay!

# CLICHÉ NO. 10

## WHEN PIGS FLY

"Southerners" are different from "Yankees" (more ways than one).

Southerners are easy going, simple, slow talking, with a Southern drawl. We got to be that way, I think, because of the hot, humid weather. We don't want to get worked up and get all hot and bothered and sweat a lot. So we take it easy.

Yankees are the exact opposite. They are always in a rush, running to catch a subway or a taxicab. They are complicated, hard to understand in speech and in manners. They talk fast and choppy. They got to be that way, I think, because of their weather (icy, cold, frigid, and miserable in the winter). They have to get worked up to keep from freezing.

When I went to the army, fresh out of high school, fresh out of the cotton fields, I met my first Yankee. He was a little, dried up, shrimp of a fellow from Brooklyn, New York, of all places!

Can you picture the scene? A Yankee from Brooklyn and a southern boy fresh off the farm from Iva, South Carolina having a conversation. The Yankee was talking ninety miles an hour and the southern boy (me) tried to speak but he couldn't get a word in edge wise. Besides that: I couldn't understand a word he was saying. So, I said: "Huh." He said: "Huh, hell, pay attention", and he kept right on talking like a "rat a tat" machine gun. I still couldn't understand, but I was afraid to say: "Huh" again!

Yes, southerners are slow, easy going people. That's why we always shorten people's names with nicknames, and why we invent phrases and speak with clichés like: "When pigs fly".

We know that pigs don't actually sprout wings and fly; but they can run so fast that their feet barely touch the ground. We call that "flying".

I never could run very fast, myself. I'm not built for running. I'm too far off the ground. I'm tall, with long legs, skinny and somewhat clumsy; but there was one occasion that I won a race. I had to win.

When I was young, a very long time ago, I was in the CCC Camp at Clemson. Another boy, who was short, sassy and spry, and I decided to go to town to see if we could meet some girls to fool around with and maybe go to a movie or something (that was before they had shopping malls).

It was a pretty good piece to town, maybe four or five miles, and we had to walk. Well, on the way, a truck passed us. The short boy with me knew the driver. So the truck stopped up the road, and the short boy took off running. I knew that he was trying to beat me to the truck, and I knew that if he beat me that he would jump on the truck and leave me stranded!

At first, I tried to match his short steps, steps for steps, but I found myself lagging. So I stretched out my long legs and gave it all I had. I was taking only one long step to his two or three short steps and I was keeping up with him. I knew that I couldn't keep that pace up for long. But I psyched him out! He became exasperated and gave up the race and started walking, and I was glad. He said: "You long legged thing you. I can't beat you"!

If I had known then, what I know now, I would have let him beat me and I could have turned around and went back to camp. There were no girls to be seen in town. It was a dry run and we had to walk all the way back to camp.

One time, I was an eyewitness to another boy who could fly: He was my son, George. When George was a little boy, about eight or nine, he and another son, Walter, were up in a tree outback from where I was working. I saw them in the tree and I decided to take a break and have some fun.

I hid in the bushes and let out a mournful cry: "OOOH! OOH! OOH!

Little George came down out of that tree and ran to where he thought I was working crying out: "Daddy! Daddy! Daddy!"

He thought "boogers" were going to get him, for sure! His feet were barely touching the ground. He was flying!

I saw how frightened he was, so I rose up from behind the bushes, and the little fellow sure was relieved. He said: "It's daddy." I gave him a hug and we both laughed.

Today, the media would call that "child abuse" to scare your "younguns" like that. But, back then, we thought it was fun. Most daddies did it.

Is it child abuse for your child to be rescued from what he thinks is a dangerous situation, and, then, be wrapped in arms of love. You be the judge.

George could flat fly, like a pig.

They have pig races at county fairs. Spectators turn out in big numbers to watch the pigs race around a track. The winner gets a prize: Some good vittles. And the pigs know it. So, they run, run, run, like a house on fire, to get there first. I've seen the races. Those pigs fly!

Hey you "Yankees", just in case you don't know it, flying can mean: "running like a streak of lightning", or "getting on down the road", or running like a "lickety split", or running "like a bat out of hell"!

# CLICHÉ NO. 11

## LIKE GREASED LIGHTNING

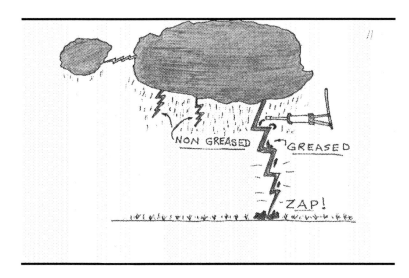

I knew a boy once who was nicknamed "Lightning". But he didn't live up to his name. He was a slowpoke. He never, ever got in a hurry. I think if his britches got on fire that he would walk to a water spigot to put the flame out. That's how slow he was.

That's probably the reason he got the nickname "Lightning". Some southern buddies saw how slow and laid back he was and they were just kidding when they started calling him lightning. But the nickname stuck.

And I know of another fellow they called "Lightning". He was puny, and skinny, and had a bad cough. He died young with emphysema. That was way back when men, and a few women, smoked stud horse, golden grain, or country gentlemen, roll your own tobacco.

Times have changed since then. There aren't nearly as many smokers today, especially, roll your own smokers.

But, "lightning" and "greased lightning" mean two different things down South.

It's not a compliment to be called "lightning" down south. But, if someone calls you "greased lightning", thank him. It's a big complement!

The sad part about being from the south is there are a whole lot more people called "lightning" than they are called "greased lightning". Again, I think the climate has something to do with it.

I have never been called "lighting" myself. I've been called "lazy bones", which means the same thing.

I remember, one time, again, a long, long, time ago, when I was a boy, I didn't want to go pick cotton (not just one time; but many times). My "paw" came up the stairs with his razor strop in hand, as was usual his custom for arousing us sleepy head boys. We heard him coming, and we didn't want that razor strop planted on our naked butts. So, we jumped out of bed and made a mad dash for the stairs.

This time, after "paw" came back down, I grabbed my belly, and bent over, and let out a groan, like my belly was sure 'nough hurting. My belly wasn't actually hurting, but my back was, when I thought about having to pick cotton!

"Paw" said: "get back to that bed, you lazy bones." I almost ran back up those stairs and jumped in that cozy bed. I knew that "paw" wasn't going to make me pick cotton, if he thought there was a chance that I was sick.

If my buddies had heard about this, I'm sure that one of them might have started calling me "lightning". I could take "lazy bones"; but, I sure would have hated to be called "lightning"!

The south is not the only place that has people who qualify for the nickname "lightning". The world over has people like that.

I'm convinced that the reason a lot of countries are poor, second rate countries, is because they have many "lazy bones" or "lightning" whose bellies hurt when they think about going to work! The Virgin Island is such a place.

I was there, once, doing some work on an airport, when I was an engineer with the FAA. Although we offered good salaries, for doing simple, easy work, we couldn't find workers. Oh, some would work a day or two; but, their bellies would start hurting and they would call in sick. Most of them would stay out for days on end. "Lazy bones" or "Lightning" was what they were! The world is full of them.

Not many people qualify for the title "greased lightning" There are a few, but not many.

I watched the Olympics that took place in Greece. I was amazed at some of those athletes. I don't see how they do the gymnastics, the high dives, the "butterflies", the sprints!

Did you see the "long jump" competition? One American, I don't remember his name (ain't it a shame!), sailed through the air 28ft 2 &1/4inches before landing in the sand. How did he do it?

And I'm proud of another American, again, I don't remember his name and what a shame! He was from Baylor University. He won the Gold Medal in a "foot race". What's so amazing was he was tall and lanky (like me), and he was white. He ran like greased lightning, or like a streak of lightning, or like a bat out of hell. He was amazing, amazing, amazing!

What this country needs, and the whole world, is for more people to get off their butts and be like those athletes (work like the world is on fire for it soon will be!!)

# CLICHÉ NO. 12

## SLOW AS A TURTLE

A turtle is a slow creature. I guess the reason that he is so slow is because he carries a heavy load. Man, I would hate to be a turtle, wouldn't you, with that shell on my back all the time? I would rather be a snake, or a weasel, or a skunk (naw, I'm just kidding. I would rather be a turtle than a skunk). But, if I were a turtle, I would want to cast that shell off and run and dance and sing and be free of that heavy load.

A turtle is a sad creature. I have never seen one smile. Dogs smile and wag their tails. Chicken hens smile and cluck and sing. Even old jack asses smile and show their teeth and go "honk", "honk", "honk", "honk".

Look around. Everything in nature is smiling: dogs, chickens, jack asses, birds, politicians, everything except turtles and "old grouches". What a shame it is!

I sure would hate to be a turtle, or an old grouch! They are never happy about anything. An old grouch could do something about his situation. He chooses to be the way he is, but a turtle is saddled with his load for life, and he can do absolutely nothing about it.

Another reason that I think a turtle moves slowly is because he has no place to go. If he chooses to cross a road, laughing teenagers, in a convertible, out joy riding, might run over him and smash him to bits and then some ugly buzzard will swoop down and peck up the pieces.

If the turtle decides to take a swim, as many of them do, laughing fishermen, high on beer, playing hooky from Sunday School, might hook him in their trot lines and make turtle stew out of him (turtle stew does go pretty good with beer and crackers).

And , if the turtle decides to take a nap, under a bridge, in the shade, where it's cool, some laughing little boys, looking for tadpoles, might find him and beg their daddies to let them keep the turtle, and take it home with them in a sack and feed him canned cat food, and try to make a pet of the turtle.

A turtle's life is much worse than a dog's life. When someone says: "He lives a dog's life", meaning: he lives a life full of hardships and burdens. It would be more appropriate to say: "He lives a turtle's life". A turtle is burdened from day one. That's why he moves so slowly.

If I were a turtle, I would swim way, way out into the ocean and get away from this cruel world, and many do just that. They come to shore only once in a blue moon to lay their eggs. Then, back to the sea they go, like some old, hen pecked seamen, old tars, old salts. This world moves too fast for them, too!

I wish this world wouldn't move so fast. I wish it would slow down and be more like a turtle. There's no need to be in such a hurry. There's no place to go. Well, there's only two places to go.

If we move too fast, we might end up, like the turtle, in a boiling fire. The other place requires that we slow down a little.

# CLICHÉ NO. 13

## IN A STILL SMALL VOICE

I wish that I could be cool in all situations. Some people have that gift. They hold their cool and never get offended by anything that someone might say about them. But, not me! If you say something bad about me, to my face or behind my back, I might smack you (naw, I'm just kidding. At one time, I would, but not anymore. I have aged a bit and got somewhat mellow). But I still get angry, sometimes. I'm working on it, though.

I guess I inherited my temper from my "paw". I have seen him, when I was a boy, get mad at mama, turn red in the face, curse, slam the door, kick the dog, and get in his "A model Ford" and leave and stay gone for a long time. When he came back, he had forgotten why he had got mad, for he was as high as a kite on "white lightning".

Usually, "paw" got mad at mama when she started nagging him about his little cotton money. She wanted some of it and "paw" wanted to keep it.

He thought that mama's cotton mill money was enough for her, and that the little cotton money, that he got farming, was his.

He did mellow, somewhat, in his later years and was more generous with his money.

Some people go through life and don't ever learn (until they get old) that it is more blessed to give than it is to receive.

I'm glad that I learned, a long time ago, that money does not buy happiness. Now, if I could only learn, and get it through my thick head, that a quick temper doesn't buy happiness either. My world, and those around me, would be happier.

But, it's like I said: I have learned, thanks be to God, sometime back, that it is blessed to give. I have received many blessings, a lot of love, a lot of contentment, a lot of satisfaction, deep down in my soul, through giving (I could give you some examples; but, I don't want to pressure you, too much, to share your "little cotton money" while you still have time).

But, I still have not completely learned to be "cool" in all situations. I still get mad, and raise my voice at stupid drivers, at stupid umpires, at stupid politicians, at stupid people all around me that don't agree with everything I say.

But, one of these days, if I keep working on it, I might be able to hold my tongue, and not get quite as angry, and not raise my voice quite as often, and be "cool".

I know that it sure would be good to keep my cool and be giving, and humble, and meek, and kind, and speak softly with a still small voice like someone I know that I met, awhile back.

He's the coolest person around. He's the humblest person around. He's the most giving person around. He will give you the shirt off his back, or his cloak. If you ask Him to walk a mile with you, He will walk two miles with you.

I'm trying to get to know him better. He's my hero. He's my role model. If I ever got to be like Him, you will know it! For I might give you everything I have and take off to be with him forever. Wow! Oh glorious day!

If I wasn't so hardheaded and stubborn (like a mule), I could be more like Him. He's just a country boy, a carpenter's son, from a little town called "Nazareth", a town not much bigger than my hometown of Iva, South Carolina.

Why don't you come and join me? We both can get to know him better! People will listen to us a whole lot better if we speak, like he does, in a still small voice, instead of the way we speak sometimes, ranting and raving.

Don't you agree that would be a cool thing to do?

# CLICHÉ NO. 14

## MAKE HAY WHILE THE SUN SHINES

Life is short. We're here today and gone tomorrow. We should make everyday count for something. We waste too much time doing things that don't amount to anything.

If I could live my life over, I would make many changes. I bet you would say the same thing. Most people would. But a lot of the things that happened in my life I couldn't help. They were meant to be. They were omens for me. They were God's plan for my life. I can look back and see it, now. I bet you can too.

Like, for me, I couldn't help being born poor, in a southern "dirt farmer's" family, with ten children (five girls and five boys). I couldn't help that. That was God's plan for me.

But listen: "God does not make mistakes. We humans err, but God doesn't. If I had been born rich, and it's God's plan for some people, with a silver spoon in my mouth, with plenty of Money, money enough to buy anything I chose to buy, I never would have had the opportunity to learn that I should: "make hay while the sun shines"! Now, wouldn't that have been a terrible shame?

If I had been born rich, I probably would have been like another fellow that I know who was born rich. He never had to hoe cotton, pull fodder, plow a mule, and slop the hogs, like I did when I was a boy. His daddy was not a dirt farmer, like mine. His daddy was a mule trader. Mule traders, back then, made a lot of money. They were kinda like our used car dealers, our pawnshop brokers, internet traders. In other words: they were "wheeler dealers".

That boy's daddy had a big plantation, with colored hired hands that did all the hard work, and a big barn in the city where he bought and sold mules and other animals.

That rich boy never got his hands dirty like I did (and calloused, too, from the hard work "paw" made me do). That boy didn't know what it meant to make hay while the sun shines. He didn't know how to work.

After his parents died, and left him all their money, he spent it like it was going out of style. He bought himself fancy clothes, fancy cars, fancy women (his women came and went), and he threw big, gigantic parties where wine and liquor flowed.

When the money ran out, he sold the mules. He sold the big barn. He sold the plantation. He sold all that his parents had left to him. His wife left him, for another man who had lots of money, she was a "gold digger", and he was flat broke!

The last time I saw him, he was nothing more than a bum. He came into this beer joint, where I was sitting on a stool having a cool "Bud". He bought a six pack, on credit, and got in his old dilapidated car, a forty nine Chevrolet, with a rusty top, and with the muffler tied up with hay baling wire, that smoked like a chimney, and drove off. I had never seen such a pitiful sight in my life.

I used to envy that boy. I thought he had it made. But now, I'm glad that I was born poor and that my "paw" taught me how to work. I'm glad that I was born like an old cow hand from the Rio Grand. In other words: "Just a plain ole southern farm boy"!

Hard work ain't never hurt anyone, except maybe little ole lazy bones boys, or maybe men who never had to work a day in their lives when they were young, those that were born with silver spoons in their mouths.

Make hay while the sun shines. It's too late to make hay after the sun goes down. It's too late to teach an old dog new tricks. It's too late to close the gate after the mules are out.

# CLICHÉ NO. 15

## DYNAMITE COMES IN SMALL PACKAGES

I have known a couple of dynamites in my life. Both of them were small, and puny, and skinny. Neither one of them could have hurt a fly. I guess that's the reason that they got the nickname "Dynamite".

I have known a few others, also, that would have qualified for that nickname, but they were called something else.

One of them was a little "bitty" fellow named "Clarence". He was a "ball of lightning". He was an "atom bomb". He was a "stick of dynamite". He was "mean as a snake". No one had better mess with Clarence when he was "high as a kite".

Some folks, who did not know about his reputation, did mess with him, though, and he left a trail of mangled bodies. Some had gun shot wounds, some had broken jaws, and some had their guts cut out.

Clarence should have been called "dynamite" instead of those other two puny fellows. He certainly qualified for that nickname.

Clarence was always ready to fight (like a bantam rooster, with his chest stuck out). He didn't have to have an excuse. It might be that he just didn't like your looks, or that he didn't like your name, or that you didn't offer to buy him a beer. He would find an excuse, if he didn't like you!

Another person who qualified to be called lightning: She was a "hot potato"; she was a "red hot mama"; she was a "Jezebel". Her real name was "Mamie"!

Mamie ruled her household. When she barked, her husband jumped. And he jumped a lot. He was what you call: "Hen Pecked". When she called, her children came running. It wasn't like at our house. When my mama called, we boys pretended not to hear her, half the time, because we knew that she would have a chore for us to do.

Mamie was a little bitty, skinny woman with red hair and freckles. She must have been fresh over from Ireland. She had a temper like the Irish.

I was afraid of her, and I wouldn't dare to look her in the eye, when I was a boy. I was afraid that she might snap my head off. She reminded me of a snapping turtle!

Mamie was like a keg of dynamite. She had a short fuse, and she was ready to explode, anytime. She should have been called "dynamite"!

I don't know why that most little bitty people are like that. Most of them strut around, with their chests poked out, like a little bantam rooster who thinks he's the ruler of the barnyard. Haven't you noticed? And, most of the time, when the little bantam comes strutting around, other chickens would scatter in all directions, except for the "fighting gamecock". He will stand his ground.

He just doesn't just talk a good fight, or crow a lot about how mean he is, but he will fight a good fight! He's the real "dynamite"! It's the same with people. The ones who do the most talking are not always the smartest. The ones who do the most listening are usually the ones with the most brain power!

If bantam roosters, that strut around with their chests stuck out, meet a real, southern bred, fighting gamecock, the bantams will drop their wings, suck in their chests, and take off running , like a scared rabbit, and try to find a place to hide, like I did, sometimes, when a fight was going on at Mamie's house!

There was another little fellow that came to Iva once, that reminded me of a bantam rooster. He was with a carnival. A lot of carnivals came to our town, back then. Most of the carnivals sold patent medicine which consisted mostly of alcohol with brown sugar mixed in. The medicines were good for whatever ailed you, whether it be consumption, lumbago, or just a plain "stoved up" feeling! These medicines must have done the job for the carnivals sold many bottles.

But getting back to the fellow, with the carnival that strutted around like a bantam rooster: His title was "The Red Baron". He was a prize fighter; at least, he thought he was.

The carnival had a big tent. The ticket price was a dime to get inside. We mill hill boys didn't have a dime, but we usually managed to slip in, with a little help from grown-ups who were inside. They would lift the bottom of the tent for us!

The Red Baron, the prize fighter, danced around, shadow boxing, like a bantam rooster, and challenged anyone from the audience to a fight. If anyone dared to get in the ring with him and lasted for three rounds, the challenger would get a prize.

I remember one fellow, a big clumsy ox, who thought he was tough (I hope you family members don't mind telling who it was) by the name of Gus Harris took the Red Baron up on his offer.

Gus climbed through the ropes (I can see him, now. I had managed to slip in). He put the gloves on, and waved, like mad, to the crowd (there was a crowd), and proceeded to box with the Red Baron (if you could call it boxing).

Gus would draw back his fist, and swing a hay maker from the floor, and try to knock the Red Baron out with one punch! The Baron saw it coming. He would dodge the blow, and would dance around, on his toes (he was a good dancer), and "peck", "peck", "peck", he would hit poor ole Gus about fifty times before Gus could try to swing another haymaker. Gus didn't last the first round (his face looked like it had gone through a sausage mill, and the referee stopped the fight)!

The next night was a different story: The Red Baron strutted to the center of the ring and challenged anyone from the audience to a fight (I had slipped in again, and my little heart was throbbing with excitement. I enjoyed seeing a fight! And I still do). This time, a different fellow, but a big man, stood up and said: "I'll fight you"! And he climbed into the ring.

The Red Baron began his dance, like a bantam rooster around the ring, covered his face with his gloves with only a slight opening to peek through, when suddenly! Wham! Out of nowhere! The big fellow landed a terrific wallop in the midsection (above the belt, in case you are wondering) and the Red Baron hit the floor! He bounced back up, but in no time, he was down again, and the fight was over! This fellow (I wish I could remember his name, but I can't) whipped the Baron and won the prize. I was proud of this man! The whole town of Iva was proud of him!

Well, the next night (I had slipped in again), when the Red Baron challenged anyone from the audience to a fight, that same fellow stood up and said: "I'll fight you"! The Red Baron, like a bantam rooster with a gamecock after him, dropped his arms, let the air out of his belly and drooped his chest, and refused to fight!

That was the end of the show. The Baron lost his job.

# CLICHÉ NO. 16

## THE SQUEAKING WHEEL GETS THE GREASE

Wagon wheels squeak, even if they have just been greased. Old wagon wheels squeak, and wobble, and clank. That's the reason farmers always greased the wagon wheels before going to the woods to get a load of firewood, or before taking a load of cotton to the gin, or before hauling the women folks to church (they put straight chairs in the wagons for the ladies).

Farmers, in the old days, used wagons and mules to haul everything. They were used about as much as we use pickup trucks today (almost every day, except during plowing season). You could tell which wagons that were used a lot by looking at the wheels. If you saw fresh grease oozing out from around the hubs, that meant that the farmer kept his wagon wheels greased. He used a five gallon bucket of grease to do the job (it took a lot of grease for the big wagon wheels).

"Paw" kept the bucket under the shelter beside the wagon. My "paw" would grease the wagon wheels after he had used the wagon. He would take each wagon wheel off and slap grease in the hub, using his fingers, and the wagon would be ready for the next haul.

Lazy farmers, who did not use their wagons (and mules) much, would let the wagons sit in the barn shelter until the grease on the wheels became black, and, caked, and hard. They would only grease the wagon wheels, once in a blue moon, and you could tell. The wheels would wobble, and squeak, and clank. And they wouldn't last long.

I have seen farmers at the gin house, with cotton to the very top of the side bodies, packed down and heavy (quite a load for mules and wagon), and the wagon wheels had not been greased in a long time. Always, during cotton picking time, there would be some farmers who neglected to grease the wheels on his wagon.

Even though I was just a little ole bare footed country boy, I knew that you should grease the wagon wheels after every use. "Paw" might have been just a poor dirt farmer, but he had a little sense, and he had taught me that much.

If you don't grease the wheels, they are going to wobble out the holes in the hubs, and finally, bam! The wheels are going to run off, and I don't have to tell you: If you happen to have a load of cotton on the wagon, you will have a problem!

I can see the scene now: A farmer with a load of cotton on a wagon, packed down to the very top. The wheels have wobbled out the hubs and finally, one of the wheels came off and went flying down across the pasture. The farmer sends his younguns chasing the wheel to bring it back so he could put it back on the wagon. But what a chore it is to jack up one side of that wagon (which is loaded with 1500 pounds of cotton, enough to make a 500 pound bale).

Don't you know that it would have been a whole lot less trouble , and a lot less work, for the farmer and his younguns, if the farmer had kept the wagon wheels greased after every use (if he, at least greased the wheel that squeaked the most).

We don't use wagons and mules anymore. They are long gone. There are not many cotton farmers, with bare footed younguns, down south anymore. They, too, are long gone and things of the past (In fact, the south ain't what it used to be).

But we still have wheels that squeak!

They are, sometimes, big wheels, that's what we call folks who are uppity, folks with a lot of ego, big shots, fat cats, wheeler dealers, activists, parasites, extremists.

We have a lot of these wheels, more so today than when I was just a little ole country boy.

Most of these wheels have never worked a day in their lives. They make a living with their big mouths and by getting their palms "greased".

They are "rabble rousers", "self appointed (but in the news ) watch dogs", "mediators", negotiators", "antagonizers", "agitators", malicious, warring, hostile, contrary, opposing, disobedient, un American, spiteful (I've done run out of words, but I know you know who I'm talking about).

The news media has built them up, given them lots of free publicity, and made them "Big Wheels" and famous.

Don't you think it's time that we quit greasing the palms of these so called "big wheels" and put some axle grease on their asses? (I'm not talking about mules, here)!

The grease that we should use (and gallons of it. It will take a lots to get their attention) should contain "red hot" pepper mixed with the grease. So that when it's applied, it will set their butts on fire, shut their mouths, stop their squeaking, and cause them to go jump in a lake, or blast them off to outer space Hey! I think I just invented a new cliché in there, somewhere!

# CLICHÉ NO. 17

## THAT'S THE WAY THE BALL BOUNCES

Professional athletes are over paid. That's the way the ball bounces.

Politicians, in most cases, are wind bags. That's the way the ball bounces.

Criminals don't get the punishment they deserve. That's the way the ball bounces.

Doctors and hospitals charge too much. That's the way the ball bounces.

And it's a crying shame! All of 'em.

We need to do something about that bouncing ball! We need to puncture it, and deflate it, so that it will come down to earth and quit bouncing!

But, how on earth are we going to get all the people together, united as one, and combine our forces so that we can defeat that bouncing ball???

It won't be easy! I can assure you of that. But, I do have a theory about how we can do it.

Allow me to explain my theory: The ball did not start bouncing on its own. It had to have had some help. Balls don't bounce without someone picking them up, and dribbling them. And who dribbles balls? Idle hands, that's who. People who do not have anything better to do. They're the ones who started the ball bouncing.

Let's go back and take a look at history, and see if we can learn when the ball started bouncing in the first place.

I think that it was during World War II that the ball started bouncing. Before that, there were no idle hands; therefore, the ball did not get bounced. Before World War II, everyone had to work in order to eke out a living to keep from starving.

There were a few professional athletes, but they did not make fabulous salaries compared to working people. Professional athletes played because they loved the sport and not because of money.

The reason the professional athletes did not make much money was because there were not that many fans who were willing to dish out their hard earn money to attend games. And, another thing: There were not that many people who could take time off from there jobs to attend games during the week. They could only go to games on Saturdays. (There were no games on Sundays because we had "blue laws", back then).

The money was not there to pay athletes big salaries. Therefore, that ball did not get bounced!

What about the politicians? Politicians were not as big wind bags before World War II as they are today. The reason was that only those politicians with proven honesty and morality were the ones elected. Society set higher standards for politicians, back then, than they do today. Therefore, that ball did not get bounced!

And Criminals? They paid the price for their crimes. There were chain gangs, and rock quarries, and jails without air conditioning and without day rooms and TVs. Criminals had to serve their time, and when they got out of jail, they did not want to ever go back. A few did go back to jail, but not as many as today. That ball did not get bounced!

Doctors and hospitals had to charge reasonable fees, before World War II, because the government did not tax the people to death, and did not give free medical care to everyone (even to the lazy "lay-abouts') as the government does today. Back then, people had to pay for their medical care out of their own pockets. Doctors and hospitals had to accept what they could get. Medicare, Medicaid, and big insurance companies came into existence after World War II. Therefore, that ball did not get bounced!

After I considered all of this, I reached the following conclusion: The only way to keep the ball from bouncing is for us to return to the era when there were no idle hands (and it's coming).

Oh God have mercy! We have it too good! The Lord has blessed us with too much! We are not good caretakers of all that He has given us! We are spendthrifts! We are lovers of selves more than we are lovers Of God! We are idlers. That's what we are!

The only way to stop that ball from bouncing is: To fast and pray, and turn from our wicked ways, and bring our offerings into God's storehouse.

If we don't do it, then the Lord might do it for us! He might allow the Babylonians to come and get us and carry us away into captivity for forty eight years, as he did for His chosen people.

You better believe that will stop that ball from bouncing!!

# CLICHÉ NO. 18

## HERE TODAY AND GONE TOMORROW

Life is short; but death lasts a long, long time. Here today and gone tomorrow. Life is but a dream. Life is like a vapor. Before you know it, whiff, life is gone!

Sometimes I lay awake at night, thinking and reliving my life. I regret. I said: "I regret", I regret, I regret! All my mistakes!

I regret holding a sharp pencil under Clara Patterson at school (without her permission or knowledge that it was there) and letting her sit down on it. My, how I regret that! She could have gotten seriously injured! Although I offered my apologies to her, over and over, and, although she forgave me and assured me that she was alright, I still regret that I did such a stupid thing, until this day. I was foolish. I was not very bright. I was a stupid nut, and I admit it, and I regret it!

I regret being a ring leader of a bunch of boys at our junior/senior banquet (We were juniors. I got a little more sense when I got to be a senior), and we clapped, like mad, after Mr. Tidieman sang, in his baritone voice, an old Irish number.

After he sang, and started to sit down, we boys led the audience in applause, so long, that he had to come back and give an encore. And after the encore, we clapped again, like crazy, and he bowed, and bowed, and finally he realized that we were making fun, and he went and sat down.

As a result of this nonsense, I got an "E" on the course he taught "Chemistry" even though I had made a 100 on the final exam! I confronted him about the grade that he had given me and he said: "That's all I think you deserve Terry (He didn't even call me by my first name)!

He knew that I was the ring leader that night, and I tell you folks: "I regret it"!

I regret having an idea one time, late at night. I didn't want to go down stairs to the bathroom, so I peed out of the upstairs window. My sister, who was sitting in the living room below with her date, heard the pee spattering on the ground outside her window and told my mama and mama tore my butt up with a hickory. I regret that, and I wish I could tell mama again that I'm sorry, but she has gone to be with the Lord. Mama, I'm sorry that I peed out of the window (I hope the Lord will let her hear me)! I regret That! (Man, you don't know just how much I do regret that)!

I regret stealing watermelons out of a certain farmer's watermelon patch, some high school buddies and me. A classmate of ours (a big mouth "tell it all" female classmate) saw us and told on us.

The farmer was a stingy farmer, and he didn't want to share his watermelons with us rambunctious, thieving boys.

He came to my house, while I was napping on the sofa. He asked mama if he could speak to Amos. Mama woke me up and said there is a man on the porch that wants to talk to you. When I went to the door, my heart sank when I saw the farmer.

He told me about the girl seeing us stealing his watermelons and said that if each of us didn't give him a dollar (I told you he was stingy), he was going to get the law on us. We each paid him to keep from going to jail (And do you know what? The watermelons were green)". Talking about regretting something, I sure do regret that!

There are a lot of things, about my life, that I regret. I could name many more; but I realize that you are probably getting bored, so I will stop.

But, before I do, please allow me to say one more thing (I hope you are still reading), there is one thing that I do not regret: I do not regret the day when I realized that we are here today and gone tomorrow and there is absolutely nothing I can do about it. But today is still here, and tomorrow may never come (and it won't for many folks).

So, I say, live for today, and try not to make so many dad-burned stupid mistakes!

# CLICHÉ NO. 19

## HORSING AROUND

You can get hurt by just horsing around. So, pay attention to what you are doing, and keep your eyes upon the road and your hands on the steering wheel. (Ask my daughter, Maggie)

Maggie can testify, from experience, that it does not pay to horse around, while driving a car. She was driving my nice, nearly new, Ford Country Squire station wagon (that was quite a while ago) to school, one day. The car was loaded with her and three other children, when one of my boys, sitting in the seat behind Maggie, started horsing around.

He said something that my daughter didn't like (Maggie, you drive like you're drunk, or something like that). Maggie got angry (she had her dad's temper), so she took her hands off the steering wheel and her eyes off the road, and turned around to give that boy, who was horsing around, a big slap on the side of his stupid head!!

Well, my nice, nearly new Ford Country Squire wagon, found itself without a driver to tell it where to go. So it decided to take a cruise through the woods. It plunged, head first, off the road into a deep ravine thicket and totally destroyed itself!

Fortunately, no one was hurt (not the driver, not the son who was horsing around, and not my other two sweet little innocent children, who had absolutely nothing to do with causing the accident)!

A car needs a driver. A car cannot drive itself. If you are going to horse around in a moving car, you are asking for trouble.

Don't do it in a car!

If you feel the urge to horse around, it is best to park the car, in a country lane, or somewhere safe, get out of the car, go in the bushes, where no one can see you, and horse around all you want, and get it out of your system.

I knew a fellow, one time that had the urge to take a nap, while driving his car down Water's avenue in Savannah, Georgia, a wide four lane highway, past midnight. He had been horsing around town, bar hopping, and having fun.

Well, when he headed home, he got sleepy. He was tired from all the dancing, cutting up, and horsing around. So, he decided to take a nap. He told me this out of his own mouth, while the car was moving, I don't know how fast, but evidently, it was moving pretty fast, he lay down in the seat, and he struck several parked cars, and almost killed himself.

He spent several weeks in a hospital bed. Young people don't horse around in a moving vehicle.

A year or so ago, a car was speeding down interstate highway I 85. The driver had a girl in his lap. They were really cutting up. An eye-witness said that he thought it looked like they were having sex. (Now, talking about horsing around)! They ran head on into another car and got killed.

Young people don't do it in a moving car (horse around)!

# CLICHÉ NO. 20

## LET IT ALL HANG OUT

Golly, some people don't care how they look, anymore. Things have really changed. Every thing has changed. Nothing stays the same. Parents have changed. Teachers have changed. Preachers have changed. Even the little town of Iva has changed. We have a traffic light, now.

Parents today act like they don't care enough for their children. They let them do anything they want to do. Back when I was a youth, we couldn't get away with anything.

Back then, most boys wore overalls (I would say 99 percent of the boys wore overalls) all the time (except to church on Sundays, and some boys even wore overalls, then). We couldn't let our britches hang down, even if we wanted to.

On Sundays, our mamas made us take off our overalls and put on pants (or knickers, with elastic in the legs, at the knees. My mama bought me a pair, and I hated them. I thought those knickers made me look like a sissy).

71

I was a country boy (A bare footed country boy. A masculine, down to earth country boy. A tough and determined country boy), and I didn't want to wear anything that made me look anything but country! And knickers for a country boy?? No way would I wear them!

But mama, took a stick, and made me wear them anyway (about two or three times was all, for I admit: I was as stubborn as that mule that "paw" made me plow). When it came to taking off my overalls and putting on those knickers, you ain't never seen a boy pitch a fit like I would pitch!

One Sunday evening, mama wanted all of us, my three brothers, and me, and her, and "paw", to get dressed up and go into Iva to a tent revival.

She got out our Sunday clothes for us to wear, and there were those knickers for me! My chest fell. I felt sad. I felt low (about knee high to a duck). "Mama! I'm not wearing those knickers," I moaned. She said: "Yes you are." I said: "No I ain't." She said: "If you don't take off those overalls and put on these knickers, you are not going with us!" I said: "I don't care. I'm not wearing those silly looking things. What will all my Iva buddies think when they see me in those things?"

Well they all got dressed in their Sunday clothes, even my brothers. (My country brothers. They didn't have to wear knickers. But I felt betrayed)!!

I saw that mama meant business. But I meant business, too! They all got into "paw's" A Model Ford touring car (the car without the canvas top). I took off running, across the field and through the woods. I was going to cut them off. I knew, if mama saw me running to catch them, she would let me go!

And "sho 'nough", just as I emerged from the woods, there they were. Mama made "paw" stop the car and let me in!

I went to that revival in my overalls. And what was so good about that ordeal was: "Mama never did try to make me wear those knickers again"!

Boys, today, don't know how lucky they are! They can wear anything they want (and let it all hang out), and their mamas don't seem to care. If they want to wear shorts to church, they can wear shorts (I've seen'em). If they want to wear overalls without a shirt, they can do that, too (I've seen'em).

They can even wear pants, with the seats down to their knees. I've seen that, too (Talking about letting it all hang out: Their underwear shows, sometimes). But I wouldn't have had to worry about that problem, when I was a boy, because I didn't wear any (underwear, that is). Well, except in the winter time, mama made me wear a union suit. That's what we call "long johns" today.

Times have really changed, and I think a lot of it has to do with our mamas and daddies not being as strict today as they were back then.

I wonder sometimes, if boys back then had been permitted to let the seats of their pants hang down to their knees, would I have joined them? I think not. If knickers made me look silly, I think "letting it all hang out" would have made me look sillier. Besides, I had enough trouble keeping my overalls straps up. I'm sure that I wouldn't have wanted to be bothered with the hassle of keeping my drooping britches up, like I see some kids at the mall on Saturday nights.

# CLICHÉ NO. 21

## KEEPING UP WITH THE JONESES

I never did have much; therefore, I never did miss much. How can you miss something that you never had to begin with?

I ended a sentence with a preposition here; but I'm sure that you will forgive me. After all, I'm just a poor ole ignorant, country boy that never went to school but two days in my life. I went in my brother's place those times, when he was sick, and I didn't learn anything for I had to tell it all to him, when I got home.

Most southerners are like me (ignorant). At least, that's the impression I get when I'm talking to a Yankee. Why, I don't know half the things that those Yankees know.

For instance: I don't know how to drive in bumper to bumper, five o'clock rush hour traffic (or eight o'clock, or nine o'clock, or two am traffic), just creeping along for miles and miles; but Yankees know how to do that. I ain't got enough sense to drive in traffic like that! If I get off work at five and if I ain't home by five thirty, my wife will have already gone to the police and filed a "missing husband's report", or some kind of report like that.

Another thing those Yankees do that tells me they are smarter than me: They talk ninety miles an hour, in a brogue that I can't understand; but other Yankees understand every word that is said. And they tell such silly jokes. Jokes that I don't think are funny; but other Yankees go "Hee Haw, Hee Haw, like a Jack Ass!

When I worked with the FAA (Federal Aviation Administration), I was invited to lecture at the FAA's Academy in Oklahoma City. Can you imagine? This poor ole ignorant, southern country boy being invited to give a lecture to a group of professional people which included, of all people, many Yankees?

But I did it with my Southern drawl and all.

I had my back against the wall. I really preferred that they find a Yankee to give the lecture; but they insisted that I do it because I had written a handbook "Maintenance Of Airport Lighting And Visual Aids Systems" (A book that they planned to use in their curriculum). I had no other choice but to go and teach.

Well, as it turned out, one of my students was a Yankee from Minnesota. He raised his hand in class, and I thought he had a question. I said: "What is it, Cramer?" (That was the Yankee's last name). He said: I can't understand what you're saying. You talk so slow with your Southern drawl. I miss half you say." I said: "Welcome to the club, Cramer. You Yankees talk so fast, with your Yankee brogue, that I can't understand you either"! The poor, ignorant, country southern students (we had some of them in the class, also) just roared with laughter, and I went on teaching. I don't think Cramer missed much after then, because he made a "B" on the subject.

There was a time, though, that I tried to copy the Yankees in my speech. When I joined the army, the Yankees out numbered us Southerners (I would say about three to one). There are a whole lot more Yankees than Southerners. I got tired of the Yankees making fun of my drawl. So, I started to talk like them. As time went on, I almost lost, completely, my Southern drawl. They even quit making fun of me, and started to treat me like I was one of their own.

Well, after the war ended, and I came home from my post in Austria (I was there for six months in the occupational forces), after getting my discharge (in New Jersey), I caught a train home to good old South Carolina (The land that I love). But, I brought with me my adopted Yankee accent!

My older brother, who had been a first sergeant (I was only a corporal), was discharged before me and he beat me home.

As soon as he heard my fake accent, he said: "Listen "paw", Amos is talking like a damn Yankee!"

Needless to say, I dropped that Yankee accent pretty quickly and I started speaking Southern again, and you will never ever catch me trying to be something I am not.

I learned my lesson. I will let the Joneses (and the Yankees) keep what they have got. I will never, ever try to keep up with them again!

# CLICHÉ NO. 22

## ME AND MY BIG MOUTH

UNHAPPY AMOS MOSES PICKING COTTON

Have you ever said something, and as soon as you said it, you wished you could take it back? I have, at least a thousand trillion times. (Well, maybe not that many, but there have been many such times for me).

I was a high school freshman, and I had this beautiful, gorgeous lady teacher, who had a finger wave in her hair. She didn't know it, but I was madly in love with her. I was in love with a lot of my beautiful, polite, sweet as apple pie, teachers, back then. We had the nicest teachers in the world! And Smart too. That's the reason I'm so smart today.

Well, I had a lot of boy in me. I was mischievous. I decided to have some fun, and try to tease this beautiful, gorgeous lady teacher that had the finger wave in her hair. I made a paper airplane, and threw it, underhanded, toward her desk, when she had her back to the class.

I must say that I did a beautiful job making that paper airplane. When I turned it loose, it sailed up and around the ceiling, and around and around, before settling down on top of her desk. All the class snickered (I was proud of myself for making them laugh. Laughter was something you didn't hear much in school, back in those days). Everything, back then, was serious, and certainly paper airplanes were not allowed.

As luck would have it, as soon as I turned the paper airplane loose, my beautiful teacher, the one with the finger wave in her hair, turned around and got a glimpse (she thought) of where the plane came from (namely: me).

She said: "Amos, did you throw that plane?" I lied and said: "No Maam. It must have been Johnny"! The whole class roared. Johnny was my younger brother. He was not even in the class. Everyone in my small school knew Johnny, especially the girls, for Johnny was a Casanova, a Don Juan, and popular. Johnny couldn't have possibly thrown that plane, and the teacher knew it! (She knew that I was pulling her leg).

She said: "Amos, I know you threw that plane." I got a little peeved knowing that she had caught me red handed and that I could not wiggle my way out of it. So I picked up my books and started for the door. I was going to the office for I knew that's where she was going to send me, anyway. (Back then, you couldn't get away with anything. Teachers would send you to the office for the least little thing. And the principal knew how to use a razor strop on the hind ends of boys).

But I wasn't scared. I was a big boy, big enough to take any punishment that they could dish out (that's what I thought).

My lovely teacher saw me with my books in my hand and headed for the door. She said: "You can go to the office"! I said: (And Lord I shouldn't have said it. Lord I'm sorry) "Hell, that's where I'm going"!

She followed me to the office and told the principal all about it (even told him that I said hell).

Instead of giving me the razor strop on my hind end, he expelled me from school for a week.

I went home and "paw" made me pick cotton (it was fall of the year and cotton picking time). For a solid week, I had to pick cotton for saying "hell" to my beautiful teacher, the one with the finger wave in her hair.

You better believe it. I never, ever made another paper airplane in school, and you better believe that I never, ever said "hell" again either. "Hell" was what I got!!

Me and my big mouth, I learned the hard way to keep it shut. I didn't want to go to the cotton patch again!

# CLICHÉ NO. 23

## THE PROOF IS IN THE PUDDING

Desserts in the old days of yore, consisted mainly of some sort of pudding: 'nana pudding, bread pudding, chocolate pudding, plum pudding, and at our house: rice pudding with raisins. I didn't particularly go for the rice pudding. My favorite was 'nana pudding with vanilla wafers in it. We had lots of 'nana pudding at our house on Sundays. Sunday was the only day that we got dessert. Today, no meal, except maybe breakfast, is complete without desert.

Have you ever been to one of those fancy restaurants where they roll out desserts on a cart and let you look at the different varieties? (All kinds: pies, blackberry, strawberry, apple, peach, blueberry, etc. and cakes: chocolate, coconut, carrot, upside downs, check-a-boards, multi-layered, etc. (No wonder we see so many obese people in the world today)!

In the "cotton picking days" of the Old South, there were not many fat people. The reason, I think was because we didn't eat desserts, except on Sundays. And then our desserts were not as fattening as they are today. On weekdays, we had only one item for dinner. For example: If were going to have crowder peas, that was it, and nothing else, except for cornbread.

Another reason one didn't see as many fat people, especially down South, in the old days, was because we worked our tails off!

I remember when I got married. I married a beautiful fraulein from Austria. She was my war souvenir. I sent for her and she came over on a Liberty ship. I met her in New York and brought her home to South Carolina via railroad. That must have been quite a change for her, although she never talked about it, coming from the big city, Linz, Austria, to Iva, South Carolina, and becoming a farm girl. Looking back, I know that was a big adjustment for her to make.

Back then, The South was still a land of farms. I farmed, for a season, after she arrived. My brother, "Dub", had a farm (Of all things: A cotton farm)! I helped him farm (Some people never learn. Do they?)

But that's what I did for a season, before I came to my senses, and told "Dub" that he could have his cotton farm that I had enough. I was gonna go to college and be an enjuneer!

And, hey! I did become an engineer. (A helleva engineer! Georgia Tech engineers had nothing on me. My cohorts called me "Famous Amos" after I wrote a book on maintenance of airport lighting systems; but that is another story).

Let's get back to that season that I farmed after my sweet little fraulein arrived from Austria: I worked my butt off (I mean literally). I did not have a butt!! You could see my tail bone, when I was naked.

Another reason that I didn't have a butt was because I was nearly starved to death. My sweet, beautiful, Austrian fraulein (bless her heart) didn't know how to make biscuits, chicken and dumplings, country fried steak, or any of that stuff.

I remember that she asked my mama how to make biscuits. My mama said: "Oh, all you have to do is take a little dough, roll it in your hands, and then roll it out with a rolling pin, pinch off a bit, and round it out to a biscuit, put it in a pan and stick it in the oven.

Then, my pretty Austrian fraulein wife, asked mama: "What is dough?"

But, like I said, I quit farming and I went to college under the G.I. Bill. Up at Clemson, my wife met some good, church going, Southern ladies that knew how to cook "Southern Style". (My wife was not only beautiful, but she was also smart. She learned quickly how to cook many Southern dishes (even better than my mama)!

I started eating her good cooking and I got my butt back bigger than ever. I liked her cooking. Her 'nana pudding was the best that I ever tasted. If you wanted to see proof that I liked it, you only had to look at my big butt. The proof is in the pudding.

And the mashed "taters", and the country fried steak, and the Southern fried chicken, and the fried apple pies, etc.

# CLICHÉ NO. 24

## CLEAN AS A WHISTLE

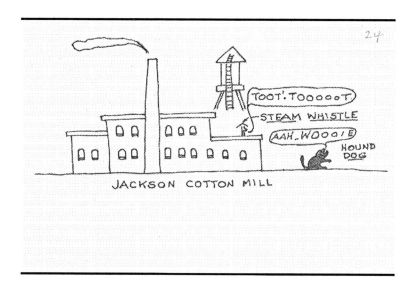

I like to see little boys and girls try to whistle. When they are first learning, they suck in, instead of blowing out, to make a whistle. That's the only way they can whistle, at first. But, they keep trying, day after day around the house (and they drive everyone nuts, except their daddies who are trying to teach them to whistle). Then, one day they master the art.

I learned to whistle, when I was real young. (I can imitate a Mocking bird, a Bob White, A Blue bird. Most all birds). I roll up my tongue and put it against my bottom teeth, and bring my lips together, except for a little hole. I then take a deep breath, and then blow real hard through my rolled up tongue and through the hole in my lips, and I make a shrill whistle (My dog can hear me from a mile away, even though he may be down by the creek, or off in the woods, chasing squirrels, or just lying under a shade tree taking a nap (which is his favorite past time).

When he hears my whistle, he comes running, jumping up and down, with his tongue hanging out, his tail wagging, gasping and panting, ready to eat (He knows that my whistle means: "It's Chow Time)!

I don't go around whistling, all the time, like some "idiots". When I whistle, it means something, like the whistle at Jackson's mill in Iva meant something. When that whistle blew, the whole mill village, all the people in town, and all the mill workers knew that it was "Chow Time": Twelve o-clock sharp.

The mill whistle blew everyday, except on Saturdays and Sundays. No work was done on those days.

Saturdays was a day of leisure. That was a day of excitement for the little town of Iva. Saturdays was the time to go to the mill ball park and watch textile league baseball. Back then, every mill town had a baseball team, and some good ones, too, and great crowds would turn out to watch baseball.

Iva had a nice park, with a big grandstand, with long rows of seats, and with a roof overhead to keep the blazing sun off the heads of spectators. Just about all the men and boys, and a few women and girls would come to the games.

The reason that there were only a few women and girls at he games was because they didn't want to see their men folks get hurt. Always, ever and always, a fight would develop between spectators, or between ball players, or between spectators and umpires at the ball games. But, that's one big reason that I went, when I was a lad. I enjoyed watching those "knock down", "drag out", fist fights (Whomp!). That was exciting!

The reason that the mill whistle didn't blow on Sundays was because the mill was shut down to allow all workers to go to church. The South was very religious, back then. Almost everyone went to church (even those that were involved in a fist fight the day before). It was against the law for factories to operate and for stores to open on Sundays. Everything was shut down. Blue Laws were enforced. It was quiet, none of this hustle and bustle that we have today.

I think that those times were better because, even though we had the fights, there was not nearly as much sin in the world.

I wish I could hear that mill whistle blow again. But that will never happen again. Jackson's mill has shut down, long ago. There are not many textile plants left in the USA today. If we want to hear a mill whistle blow, we will have to go to China, or to India, or to South America. We will have to leave this country and go someplace else where they are having all the fun!

We have forgotten how to have fun in America (Community fun). We are too busy working on Saturdays and Sundays.

That mill whistle was the symbol of an era, in my life, when people were neighborly, friendly, close knit, and loved one another.

That was a time when people might "cut up" a bit on Saturdays but would go to church and confess their sins on Sundays. That was a clean time. "Clean as a whistle" you might say.

Lord, I wish I could hear that mill whistle blow again!

# CLICHÉ NO. 25

## WATER RUNS DOWN HILL

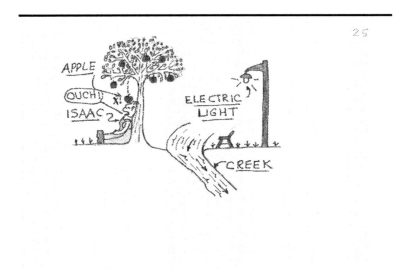

Water will seek the lowest point. I learned that, a long time ago, in Mr. Kellet's physics class. He taught us a lot of stuff about the laws of physics. He tried to teach us about the laws of electricity, but he was never much good at it. (If you are going to fool around with electricity, you better know what you are doing. Mr. Kellet didn't know a whole lot and he almost set the world on fire. Well, he almost set his desk and the classroom on fire).

He rigged up this simple AC circuit, with a light bulb, rheostat, switch, etc., and when he threw the switch, there was a loud pop. All the wiring began to smoke and became red hot. He quickly turned the switch off, and after the smoke had cleared, he rewired the circuit and tried again. When he threw the switch, he got the same result: There was a loud pop, the wires started smoking and became red hot. In disgust (you could see it in his red face), he gathered up the components, stashed them in a closet, and went on to something else (like it wasn't his fault).

Water runs downhill. Electricity will run uphill, downhill, sideways, all which-ah-ways (ask Mr. Kellet)!

Water runs downhill because of the law of gravity. This law applies to everything on earth. Everything applies to you and me and anything that occupies space and has weight (Fat people, little people, grasshoppers, politicians and other wind bags, everything). The bigger you are the harder you will fall. What goes up must come down. That's the law of gravity.

There is another law: The law of economics. I learned about this law at dear ole Clemson College, in Mr. Kirkland's class in Economics 202. This law concerns supply and demand.

Before you work hard, and spend long hours designing and making something to sell, you better test the market first to see if there's a demand for your product. If there is no demand, no matter how big an inventory you may have, your labors will be in vain.

Ask me. I know. I spent five years of my life, and my wife's life, writing and rewriting a book "Horse Sense And Birdhouses". I have my garage filled with books. After a blazing start, sells have dropped to a trickle. There's not much demand for the book. I think that it is probably due to the fact that Southerners don't have much interest in horses, and mules and fields of cotton anymore.

Horses and mules and wagons and cotton used to be popular in the South. They were hot items, but folks down here have lost interest in these things. If you want to buy a mule today, you will have to go to Missouri, or to Romania, or to some place where they still sell mules.

Blacksmiths' shops (Iva used to have two), where one could go to have plows sharpened, mules shod, or wagon wheels repaired. Blacksmiths have shut their doors and gone out of business.

And cotton gins (Iva used to have two) have vanished. The few cotton farmers that are left in the South probably have to go to China to get their cotton ginned for that's where the textile industry has gone.

Lastly, allow me to talk about another law (A law that is down in black and white, and a law that is ignored by the vast majority of people the world over): "The wages of sin is death".

That's a law, also, folks and that law will never change. Not one of God's laws ever change. As long as there is an earth, water will continue to run downhill and people will continue to die for their sins!

All have sinned. All will die. There is a price for sin: Death!

But the good news is: "Someone, who was without sin, has paid the price". He, also died, but because He was without sin, he paid the price for those who do sin. (Me, you. And all people. I learned that in Sunday school when I was a lad of about fourteen).

Hey! Ain't that good news? And it doesn't cost a cent (not a red penny. How 'bout that?)

All we have to do is face the facts: We are sinners. Face that fact. We are going to die. Face that fact. But we can live again. Face that fact. We can live again! We can live, forever! We can get out of this rat race that is leading us straight to hell. All we have to do is to ask the one who died for our sins to forgive us for our sins. That's it. That's all there is to it. Ain't that easy?

Yes, there are all kinds of laws: Law of gravity (water runs downhill); law of economics (supply and demand); law of the wages of sin is death (that's the most dangerous law of all).

Life is short. Death lasts a long, long time. That's a fact and one of God's laws. I'm really glad that I have learned about these laws. Now, maybe, I will stay out of trouble!

# CLICHÉ NO. 26

## SATURDAY NIGHT'S SPECIAL

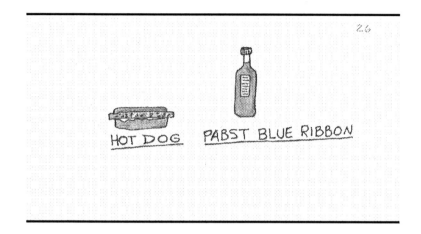

A long time ago, way back yonder when I was a boy down South, Saturday nights were a very special time. No one worked on Saturdays, except store clerks, icehouse employees, the police (they were busy), and gas station attendants (I was one. I pumped Dixie Gas. The station was owned by a fellow with the name "Gus Harris". He was the one who challenged the Red Baron, a boxer with a carnival mentioned elsewhere in this book. Hey! That has been a long time ago)!

Iva was a bustling place on Saturdays. That's when farmers from everywhere came to town to do their shopping. Crowds would gather on the streets. Men in their overalls, straw hats, and brogan shoes would play checkers, and "shoot the bull", and argue about everything under the sun, under the big magnolia tree that was located near the Iva Drug Store.

Speaking about the Iva Drug Store: There was always a peculiar odor in that place. It smelled something like cough syrup, rubbing alcohol, liniment (we used lots of it), or something else. Drug stores don't smell like that, anymore. I guess it's because

89

medicines come in pill form today, and druggists don't have to do as much pouring and mixing.

The Iva Drug Store had a soda fountain, with a marble top counter, with stools for patrons to sit while sucking on a chocolate milk shake through a straw. The fountain had long handle hand pumps and chrome goose neck spigots. There were a couple of round, wrought iron, glass topped tables in a corner where one could sit and make goo goo eyes at his girl friend (private like). I had a brother-in-law that was a "soda jerk" in that drug store (Hey! That has been a long time ago).

The Iva Drug Store was a busy place, especially on Saturdays. Another busy place was the Iva Café. The café was owned by Marice Lopez. He had a helper by the name "Frank Brown". The café smelled up the community. They sold many hotdogs smothered in onions.

Frank was the cook, and waiter, and dish washer. He did it all. My "paw-in-law" said that when Frank got real busy, and if someone ordered a hotdog, Frank wouldn't take time to use a fork to take the wiener out of the boiling water, that he would just wet his fingers with spit from his lips and grab the wiener, and put it on a bun. I don't remember ever eating a hotdog cooked by Frank. My "paw-in-law" said that he never ate a hotdog in his life.

(I guess watching Frank was the reason).

Another busy place, in Iva, on Saturdays, was the Iva Depot. The C&W C train made a daily trip. Except the train didn't run on Sunday, from Augusta, Georgia To Anderson, S.C.. The train no longer runs through Iva. The rails have been taken up and the depot has been moved. Someone made a nice home out of the depot.

But, when the train did run, it was powered by a steam engine. There was a fireman aboard, whose job was to shovel coal. For a long time, after trains stopped using steam engines and started using diesels, the railroad unions still made the railroads have a fireman aboard, even though there was no coal to shovel. I'm not a union man, myself. I guess it's because mama made me wear union suits, which I hated.

I can still see that depot, in my memory. It had a waiting room, with long wooden benches. I can see men, with their hats on, and women, too, with large wide brim hats, waiting to catch the train to go to Anderson. That was before Mr. Cook started a bus line, which put the C&W C passenger service to Anderson out of business.

I rode that train, once with my mama. We had a window open and I got black smut all over me, and around my eyes, too. Mama didn't get much smut on her. She was sitting on the other side of me, away from the window. I'm not going to tell you who I looked like, when I got off that train. But, he was little, and black, and had the initials: "SAMBO". Those were "the good old days"!

Thanks for the memories! Saturdays were exciting times for all boys, back then, and Saturday nights, too.

I remember when a bunch of us cotton mill boys gathered around Mr. Jay Burdette's Philco, magic eye, radio and listened to prize fights. Prize fights was the sport we liked, but I was never much good at boxing. Tommy Davis, who was just a skinny little runt, was the best. He could beat the socks off a big, tall, lanky, clumsy fellow by the name of "Amos Moses". Ain't it a shame?

But, we did get excited on Saturday nights listening to the fights on the radio. Joe Louis was the champ. But we usually pulled for the underdogs, who usually got beat in the first round.

Prize fights, hotdogs, and Papst Blue Ribbon Beer, sponser of the fights, were specials for us, back in those days (And I miss'em).

# CLICHÉ NO. 27

## STINKING TO HIGH HEAVEN

People used to draw water, from hand dug wells. Some folks had their wells on the back porches of their houses (all houses had back porches), where they wouldn't have to walk far to draw water. Our well was a good piece (that's distance) from the house.

All our water came from that well.

Water used for washing our faces and hands in a pan, came from a bucket, which set on a table beside the kitchen screen door. A dipper hung on a nail above the water bucket.

Water used for drinking, making tea and coffee, and for cooking, on a wood burning stove, came from that well.

Water used by mama, and a big black hired lady by the name of Mildred, to wash our filthy, dirty, sweaty, union suits, overalls, and denim shirts (on Mondays) came from that well.

Mama and "Big Mildred" would start, early, on Monday mornings, and wouldn't get through boiling, and scrubbing (using a scrub board), and rinsing (two rinses), and hanging out clothes to dry, until late in the afternoon. There were a lot of boys: five. And a lot of girls: five. And a lot of dirty clothes: Piles and piles.

Mama used a fifty gallon black pot to boil the dirt out of the colored clothes. I don't think she boiled the whites. She used four big tin tubs: two tubs with warm, soapy water for washing and two tubs with cold water for rinsing. When the water got real dirty, she would pour it out, and start over with fresh water. She used a lot of water.

It was our jobs, my brothers and I, to draw the water, tote all that water, and keep the fire burning around the wash pot.

After mama and Big Mildred got through washing clothes, we boys could jump in the water (naked) that was left over in the tin tubs and "call our selves taking a bath". I always attempted to get the tub that had the water which was used for the first rinsing. This water was cleaner and slightly warm. The water used for washing was soapy and dirty, even too dirty for me, but was not too dirty for my brothers. The water used for the last rinsing was too cold for me.

That was our Monday afternoon's bath.

Sometimes, after working in the fields all day, plowing, hoeing, picking cotton, or what ever, we would wash up at the well. We kept a tin tub up there to rinse off the red dust and dirt from our feet and legs and hands, before going into the house.

The boys usually took a bath on Saturdays, also, in tin tubs, with cold water (I mean icy cold) in the cotton house.

Mama usually took a bath everyday, before going to the cotton mill to work. She heated her bath water in a black kettle on the kitchen stove. She bathed in a closet, behind a closed door. I don't know if "paw" ever took a bath or not. I never did see any evidence that he bathed. I have seen him wash his face, in a pan and throw the dirty water out the back door. I have seen him shave, using soap in a cup with a shaving brush to lather his face, and a straight razor, that was before safety razors were invented; but I'm not aware that he ever took an all over bath. Maybe he did. He might have slipped out to the cotton house, or went down to the creek and took a bath. But I don't know, if he did.

In general, country folks didn't take many baths. It was just too big of a chore to draw all that water. Everybody, in those days, had bad B.O., except some women folks. My mama never did stink. I thought that she always smelled good. She used lots of Rose Mary, or something similar, body powders.

I remember, when I was just a wee little boy, going to school, when we lived on the mill hill, after school, I would always run home, as fast as my legs would carry me, to see my mama, and get a hug, before she went to work (She worked on the second shift). But I usually didn't get there in time. She, most of the time, had already gone to work. My heart would hurt. I loved my mama so much, and I would pick up a piece of her clothing that she had been wearing and smell it. I loved the smell of mama!

I loved my teachers, too. They were the best teachers in the world. But the love that I had for mama was special. I don't think mamas ought to work. They should stay home with their children, and hug them, and wear some sweet smelling powder, and smell like a mama!

Yes, most people stank back then. But a fellow told me that one can get used to anything, and I think he's right. He said that you could take some chicken manure, cow manure, horse manure, any kind of manure, and put it on the bill of your cap. And after wearing it for several days, you would get used to the smell and forget that you had manure on your cap.

Almost everyone had B.O. back in the "good old days", but we didn't notice the smell, because we were used to people stinking to high heaven. One fellow had stinking feet, though, that I never did get used to. One time my brother and I were at the Iva theater. I smelled someone's rotten feet. I told my brother: "Old blank, blank must be in here somewhere, because I smell his feet"! My brother said: "You better be quiet. He's sitting right behind you"! Talking about stinking to high heaven, he did!

# CLICHÉ NO. 28

## WHAT GOES AROUND COMES AROUND

Gosh, I hate to be around uppity people. Don't you? (People that will walk all over you, if you let'em) (People that act like they own the world). (People who would sell their mamas down the river). (People who think they can get away with anything)

I knew a fellow like that. He had more gall than a Christmas turkey (a tom turkey). He walked into a country store, walked behind the counter, got himself a pack of Lucky Strike cigarettes, stuck them in his shirt pocket, stood around for a while, and shot the bull with the owner, and walked out of the store without paying for the cigarettes!

There was another fellow, in Iva, that strutted around, with his chest poked out, had every hair on his head in place, wore a necktie to our country school, thought he was a ladies man, always had a smirk on his face, and he thought that he could get away with anything.

Well this uppity person, who I'm talking about, found out, the hard way, what goes around comes around.

He was up on his cloud nine and he was brought down to earth (literally) by a plain ole country dude that wore overalls, most of the time, who never wore a tie, not even to church, whose daddy was a poor dirt farmer and lived in a shack.

I know this country dude pretty well, because it was none other than me! We were seniors in high school, both of us.

If I sound like I'm bragging, it's because I am! I didn't know I had it in me. I was amazed at myself.

What brought it all on was: There was a short, you might say "puny" fellow, in my class that this uppity fellow, with the tie, was always pestering. The little fellow was my buddy. He told me about the bigger boy that was always picking on him.

I told my buddy: "Listen. If that jerk (that's what I call egoists, because I don't like them) ever hits you, let me know for I'm itching to get his you-now-what!

Well, one day, about noon, I came into my homeroom class and found my buddy with blood streaming from his nose. I asked him what happened. He said: "Amos, you have your chance. He hit me"! I said: "Don't worry, little buddy. I will get him, after school."

The message traveled like wild fire throughout the school: "There's going to be a fight, after school"! The whole student body, everyone from elementary through high school, was standing around waiting to see the fight. We waited, and we waited, and finally (at last), the doors opened and down the steps came this boy, with every hair in place, dressed fit to kill, with tie and all, with his books. I guess the reason he was late was that he had heard, also, that there was going to be a fight and he didn't want to meet his match.

I met him at the foot of the steps and I said: "Lay down your damn books." The coward was petrified. He stared, with a blank look in his eyes (Lordy, I can see him now), and he did not lay down his books. So I socked him in the mouth, and he hit the ground. He scrambled around and got to his feet and came at me. So, I let him have it again, with my left fist, and he went down, again.

"What goes up must come down". If you are uppity in this life, there's a day coming when you will be brought down. That day came, suddenly, unexpected, to this fellow.

My high school superintendent and principal were standing in the door watching. After they saw the boy hit the dust the second time, they knew there would be no fight, that it would be just me, and they didn't want to see me kill him, so the superintendent came down, laid his hand on my shoulder, and said: "Amos, you have punished him enough. Come back inside and wait for the crowd to leave and then go home."

The superintendent told me, later, that the boy's daddy had come to the school and wanted to take a warrant out for me. The superintendent told him: "If you take a warrant out for Amos, you will, also, have to take a warrant out for your son for he struck the little boy, Amos's friend."

The superintendent, and everybody else in the school, knew that boy was too uppity, and needed for someone to bring him down to earth.

What goes around comes around. (Hey! I hope you don't get the idea that I'm a fighter. That was the only fight I ever had. After that, I hung my gloves up and became a lover. It was a whole lot more fun)!

# CLICHÉ NO. 29

## BEATING AROUND THE BUSH

I'm a very impatient man. I don't like for people to try to tell me a story and go around the world, filling in every little detail, details that don't amount to a hill of beans, and then forget the punch line. How stupid can one get? That's what I ask myself. I am very impatient and unforgiving for something like that.

We have a lady in our church that fills in the details. And she does not forget the punch line. She's funny. I'm not calling any names, but her husband's name is Wayne. How she can remember all the details of the many stories she tells is beyond me.

She's full of stories, and baloney, and details. Naw, I take that back. She is not full of baloney. She's funny.

She entertained a bunch of us old folks on a bus ride from Iva, S.C. to The Dillard House in Franklin, North Carolina.

If I could remember all the details, which I cannot, I would just have to beat around the bush, I would tell you her "Bull Story". It's funny, but you need to hear all the details. It goes something like this: The bull got out of the barn and went to a neighbor's house. She went to get the bull, carrying a bucket of feed and a rope. The rope got looped over the bull's head, and the other end of the rope got looped around her body. Then, the bull took off, and took her for a ride. She plowed up every garden in the neighborhood.

The neighbor came to help. The bull took the lady down through some woods, and the bull went one way around a tree, and she went the other way. She fell to the ground and the neighbor fell on top of her. He looked down into her sparkling blue eyes and said: "I think that we had better quit meeting like this"!

Pshaw! That's all the details I remember. You better get her to tell it. She won't beat around the bush. She's funny! She's a gifted story- teller. She kept us laughing all the way from Iva to The Dillard House and back. She didn't miss a detail or the punch lines.

But some people don't know how to tell a story. They will get halfway through a story and forget the details and start to make things up. You can tell. They will roll their eyes, and stammer, and say a lot of ers, and ask someone if they remember. They beat around the bush too much, and when they do finally finish the story, everybody goes "Huh???"

I met a guy like that, once, in Le Havre, France. He was a bar tender in the hotel that I was staying, when I was on a business trip. That's back when I thought life was in the fast lane, but I have changed, since.

The guy tried to tell me a story. He spoke broken English and he talked mostly with his fingers, touching his lips, and waving his hands, and rolling his eyes. I haven't figured out till this day what he was trying to tell me. I think he was bragging about his girlfriend, who was a "Go-Go" dancer in the bar; but I'm not sure. He beat around the bush too much.

# CLICHÉ NO. 30

## PRETEND IT AIN'T SO

I used to know a guy, a construction worker, who told me a very bad story on himself. He lived in a small town, much like Iva. I'm not going to tell you the name of the town because, if you happen to be from that town, you might know whom it is that I'm talking about. Everybody knows just about everyone in small towns.

The fellow had broken his leg, had it in a cast, and had to stay home from work. His wife worked on the second shift in a local cotton mill. That's back when we still had some cotton mills left in this country.

Well, one night, his wife got off work early (whether she knew something was going on that shouldn't be going on, I do not know). But when she got home and put the key in the lock of the front door, her husband, and the woman that he had in bed with him, heard her. (Ain't that terrible?). The husband told the woman: "That's my wife. You better scat out the back door"! The woman grabbed her panties and other clothes and made a "bee line" for the back door. Just as the wife entered the room, and the back door was closing behind the naked woman.

The wife thought that she had got a glimpse of someone going out the back door; but she wasn't sure. So, she rolled up a newspaper and started beating her husband all over the head. He threw up his hands, for protection from her blows and said: "Hey! What's wrong with you"? His wife said: "You had a woman in bed with you. That's what's wrong with me!" Bam! Bam! Bam!

The man should have been a movie actor. He was good at pretending it ain't so. He said: "You're crazy. I haven't had a woman in here. You're nuts"!

Well, she couldn't be absolutely sure that she had seen someone. So, she gave him the benefit of the doubt and stopped beating him.

He told me that happened quite sometime ago, but, every once in a while, she will still say: "You did have a woman in bed with you, didn't you?" And he would say: "Naw, honey, you're the only woman in my life"! He said that would pacify her for a while and then, later, she would start thinking about it and would ask him again: "You did have a woman in bed with you, didn't you?"

He told me that he never did tell her the truth. He kept on pretending that it wasn't so for a long, long time.

I know another guy (or a couple of guys) who pretended to be something that they were not (These are true stories. I'm not making them up).

One time, in Griffin, Georgia, a man robbed a bank. He took the money and ran, on foot, to a local neighborhood. He burst into a house where a lady was home all alone, washing clothes, sweeping the floor, making beds, or doing something that lady folks do.

The robber pointed his pistol at the lady and said: "Get me some of your clothes" (He was about her size).

She went to a closet and got him a nice, blue pokey dot dress with pleats (you've seen'em), a white hat, a blue patent leather pocket book, and blue patent leather high heel shoes, which matched the dress (she wanted him to be in style), and he dressed himself in her clothes. Quite frankly, he looked ridiculous!

Then, he made her get in the car, with him beside her, and said: "Drive. I will tell you where to go."

Everywhere he told her to go, there were cops blocking the roads. He didn't feel comfortable enough to try to fool the cops. So, he told the woman to turn here and to turn there. Finally, he became exasperated and told her to stop, that he was going to get in the trunk, and for her to drive on, past the cops, pretending that everything was ok.

Well, as soon as the bank robber got in the trunk, the lady drove up to where the cops were blocking traffic, and told the cops: "I've got him. He's in the trunk"!

The moral of this story is: "A man should not pretend to be a woman for he does not know how!"

The other story that I want to tell happened in Georgia, also. It happened in a subdivision south of Atlanta.

There was a man who pretended to be a robber. Listen to this story. I swear it's true. He burst into this nice, big, upscale home, as are most homes in suburban Atlanta for most of the homes are owned by airline pilots, who are folks with lots of money. The homeowner was sitting in his easy chair, reading a newspaper, when the "would be robber" burst in. The robber threw his gun on the man and said: "Gimme your money!"

The man quit reading the paper and looked up over his glasses at the robber and said: "Hey! That's a nice gun. What will you take for it?" The "would be robber" said, without blinking an eye (I'm not making this up): "I won't take a penny less than forty dollars for the gun." The homeowner said: "I think that's reasonable. I'll buy it, but I don't have the cash. Will you take a check? My check is good. I certify it. You can take it down to the "Little General Store", at the foot of the hill, and they will cash it for you. They know me down there, and they know my check is good."

The "would be" Robber, said: "OK. I will sell you the gun." He told the man his name and the man made out a check for forty dollars and the robber went on his way to the "Little General Store" to cash the check. When he got there, and went in to cash the check, cops came in right behind him and took him to jail. The homeowner had called the cops! You can't trust anyone, anymore!

The moral of this story is: "Don't pretend to be a robber, if you don't know how, and by all means, keep your gun, don't sell it. But, if you are desperate and need the cash, and do sell your gun, by all means don't take a check, not even a certified check. Get cash for the gun. And as soon as you get the money in hand, run like a bat out of hell, out the door, before the man shoots you!"

# CLICHÉ NO. 31

## WHAT YOU SEE IS WHAT YOU GET

I've always heard that if you look like a duck, walk like a duck, and quack like a duck, then you must be a duck! But in our society, today, you can't always, sometimes tell. A long time ago, when I was a boy, this was true, but not today. If you think it's a girl, don't be too sure. It might be a boy.

There are fakes all around. There are folks that look like the real McCoy, but they are not the real McCoy. (I'm not talking about Fred McCoy. He's for real). He cannot be duplicated. He's one of a kind. They broke the mold when they made him. He's so ugly that he's pretty, with his red hair, his crooked grin, pale blue eyes that always have a twinkle, like he has something up his sleeve and he's not about to tell you what it is. He's the real McCoy. That's what he always tells folks, and I agree.

I'm sorry, ladies, he's taken. My sister has him and she's going to keep him. He's Mr. Perfect. If you don't believe me, ask my sister. One time, a bunch of women, in her church, were complaining about their husbands, and one said: "Ah, none of them are perfect." But my sister spoke up and said: "I've got one that is!" I'm glad that she thought he was perfect. I don't, not by along shot. I do think he is the real McCoy, but I do not think he is perfect. There is only one that is perfect, and he died on a cross because of the fact that He was perfect. He cannot be duplicated.

Fred McCoy is a real McCoy. But Amos McCoy is not. He's a fake. His accent in his speech is a fake. He acts like he's a country bloke, but he's nothing but a highfaluting, city slicker. He hops on one leg and limps like he is lame, but he is not. Why, I bet, he could out run a horse. The only thing real about him is: He is a grandpa. He's old enough.

Amos McCoy is not a real McCoy. He is a Hollywood McCoy. The woods are full of them around Hollywood. They are all fakes.

There is nothing real and true in movies, anymore. (Used to be, but not anymore). Hollywood has gone insane. "What you see is not what you get". Not in Hollywood.

And often, even in real life, "what you see is not what you get".

There was a famous football coach (At least, he was famous around the South). His team was one of the better teams in the South (And that's saying a lot. There are a lot of good football teams in the South: CLEMSON!! Florida state, LSU, etc.). But, this coach was not satisfied with winning in the South (Where he could have kept his job until the cows come home). He wanted to be famous Nationwide. He wanted to be on TV every week, not just once in a "Blue Moon". He wanted for people everywhere, all football fans, to sit up and listen, when he spoke.

An opening came up that would make all his ambitions come true: "Coach at Notre Dame!"(How sweet it seemed). Man, I'm going to be famous (like me "Famous Amos"). He thought. He submitted his application and resume and low and behold, he got the job!! His dream had come true! Coach at Notre Dame! The most prestigious job in America!

But it wasn't long before his ego was deflated (like a big pop of a balloon). All the wind went out of his sails. He was humiliated. He hung his head in shame. And what's more: All the

105

world heard about it on CBS, NBC, ABC, Fox, CNN, BBC, TASS and all the networks of the world!

This man had lied. He was not who he said he was. He was not the "Real McCoy". His resume did not jive with the facts. (how shameful, how disgraceful, how disgusting). He was fired from his dream job!

I wish it could be like it was in the old days, don't you? The days gone by, when people could be trusted to tell the truth, when Hollywood movies were clean, when lies were just little bitty lies, when "What you see is what you get". The world would be a whole lot better place, wouldn't it?

# CLICHÉ NO. 32

## RIDE AN OLD HORSE TO DEATH

Way back yonder. Way, way back yonder, people rode horses (and mules, and donkeys, and buggies, and stage coaches). That was, even before, "T" Model Fords, and even before coal burning, steam locomotives.

Horses were used a lot: They were used for farming, for excavation in doing road work; for buggy rides on Sundays, and were used for transportation.

Horses were, also, used for mail delivery. That's how the USA Postal Service began, via The Pony express, from town to town (rather from village to village), across America (I've seen it on TV).

Back then, mail delivery schedules were important (my, how times have changed)! "Through rain or snow, the mail must go"! That was the postal service's motto! Through dangers, toils, and snares, the mail must go. With Indians, hiding behind trees, lying in wait, and robbers, too, the mail must go!

Over the mountains and through the woods, with nothing but a trail of a road, and through deep valleys with wildebeests, mountain lions, and stinking polecats, and over the parched sands of deserts (with only one can of water. I've seen it on TV), the brave, courageous, dedicated, mail carriers rode their fleet footed horses, because the mail must go! (MY, how times have changed)!

Ranting, raving, raging Indians. with painted faces and with bands of beads on their foreheads, with eagle feathers sticking up behind their heads, with Tommy Hawks and with bows and arrows in a quiver slung across their backs, riding on pintos, roans and wild mustangs chased the mail carriers, many times, and would have scalped them had they caught them (A white man's scalp was a treasured souvenir for the Indians).

I'm proud of our frontiersmen and the Pony Express. They were always able to outrun those savages, and get the mail there on time. The mail carrier's horses were slick, fast, and built for running races, and the mail carriers were cagey. They always knew, ahead of time, what the Indians planned to do (Like: cut the mail carrier off in a dry gulch. But the mail carrier would, ever and always, get there, by the hair of his chin-chin-chin, before the Indians).

The Pony Express Riders had sworn, on a well worn Bible, that nothing was more important than people's mail, and that nothing (I said: "nothing") would stop them from getting the mail through.

Just think about it: Oftentimes, robbers, with weather beaten, scarred faces, in wide brimmed sombrero hats pulled down over their foreheads, barely above their brown, squinting, fire spitting eyes, with black, curled-up, handle bar mustaches (what a scary sight. I've seen it on TV), and with Colt 45 revolver pistols, with barrels as long as your arm, would come out of nowhere, yelling, and whooping, and screaming like wild men (I've seen it on TV, especially, along the borders with Mexico), because they had heard that there was "GOLD" in them "dar" mail pouches.

But, our brave, courageous Pony Express Riders were always able to out run, and out shoot Those Mexican villains. I can see it now (If I had my TV on and tuned to the right channel), the Pony

Express Rider on his horse, with Indian, and or, Mexican peons chasing him. His horse is flying, with his ears and mane laid back, and with his tail straight out behind him. The mail carrier is riding sidesaddle. He shoots and one Indian (or movie stunt rider) drops and falls out of his saddle (He doesn't fall completely. One leg is caught in the stirrup, and he just dangles), but the rest of the savages keep on coming.

Just in time, the Pony Express Rider arrives at the Wells-Fargo station (that's another story), where a fresh horse is awaiting. He jumps off his sweaty, gasping, panting horse and runs and mounts (leap frog style) onto the fresh horse, and off he flies, leaving his pursuing enemies to eat his dust.

That's the way folks, in the old days, rode horses. They rode them, until they were all fatigued and ready to drop.

I know that you have seen it on TV, too. And I know that you must be as bored as I am. So I'm going to stop talking about it, before I ride this old horse to death!

But I do wish that our mail carriers today would change horses every now and then, and get my mail to me on time, and not put somebody else's mail in my box!!

# CLICHÉ NO. 33

## SKINNY AS A RAIL

Beauty is in the eyes of the beholder. Beauty is only skin deep. These are clichés, and you have probably heard them, and maybe, used them, especially, if you are as old as me. Most clichés are old. Old timers used them a lot. I don't think clichés are being invented anymore.

But I'm about as old as most clichés, and she is, too, if she is still living. I don't know if she is still around, or not. But, even if she is, I don't think she would mind my telling you about us.

She was my first date (My, that has been a long time ago)! She was as skinny as a rail.

But, do you know what? It didn't matter to me, because, as for as I'm concerned, beauty is only skin deep. In my eyes she was the most beautiful thing that I had ever seen. She was my first date, my first kiss, my first girlfriend, and my first love. I fell head over heels in love with her, even though I was only sixteen.

She was in love with me, too. She wanted to get married. (At sixteen?) Where will we live? Well, we can live with mama and daddy. (Are you young folks still that crazy?)

Her daddy had a job in Jackson's cotton mill. I think that he was a loom fixer and made pretty good money, as far as cotton mill workers go.

Needles to say, I didn't have a job at sixteen years old. At least, I didn't have a money making job. I had a job, alright: Plowing a mule, hoeing cotton, sloping hogs, etc., but I didn't make any money. Paw got it all and he wasn't about to share it with no newly weds.

If that skinny girl and I had gotten married, we would (certainly), have had to live with her mama and daddy. I couldn't have brought her home with me. (Besides, I don't think that she was fed like we were, else she wouldn't have been so skinny).

At my house, we ate mostly fattening foods. We ate lots of biscuits, fat back, beans and cornbread, and drank lots of buttermilk. I don't believe that she would have liked mama's cooking, and she might have gotten even skinnier!

She was a picky eater, anyway. I remember, one time, that I invited myself to her house for Thanksgiving dinner. Her mama was a good cook (A good Southern cook). She was such a good cook that I had to think long and hard about my skinny girlfriend's proposal.

Well, at that Thanksgiving dinner, I ate like a hog. I was starved, like I stayed most of the time. I was still growing and it took a lot of food for me. But my girlfriend hardly ate. I guess she was love sick. Her mama tried to get her to eat, and her mama would try to get me to persuade her to eat, but she would just sit there, with stars in her eyes, watching every spoonful that I ate.

After dinner, she wanted for us to go out on the lawn and have her mama take our pictures. She got her camera (a black Kodac box camera. You've seen'em, if you are as old as I am), and she got some "Anderson Independent" newspapers for us to sit on. Her mama took our picture. I had my arms wrapped around her and she had her arms wrapped around me. We had our cheeks together and we were smiling like we were madly in love, and we were, deeply.

111

After the picture taking session, we got up and started to go sit in the swing on the front porch (where we sat lotsa times, talking silly talk, and kissing, and making love), and she left the newspapers lying in the yard. I asked her: "Aren't you going to pick up the papers"? She said: "Naw, let mama do it."

That hit me between the eyes like a bomb shell. That woke me up. I had blinders on up until that time. I came to my senses and realized that I could never pamper her like she had been used to being pampered. She was an only child and she got everything that she wanted, except me.

I had nine brothers and sisters. My mama didn't give me everything that I wanted. I had to battle for everything I got. That was a big difference.

When she didn't want to pick up the papers, I decided, right then, that she was not the girl for me. If I married her that I would spend the rest of my life picking up papers, taking out garbage, sweeping floors, making beds, washing clothes, etc. I would be, what you call, hen pecked. And ole masculine me didn't like the idea of being hen pecked. So, I let her go.

Shortly after that, I started dating her best friend (and fell madly in love with her, too. I guess you could say that I was just a lover boy). But, I had to let her go, too, for Uncle Sam needed me to go fight a war (that's another story).

I wish I knew what ever became of my first love. She moved away, and I lost track of her. But, I bet that she fattened up (most women do, when they get older. They call it "middle age spread"), and she probably found someone who loved her so much that he wouldn't mind picking up after her (a man that she could "hen peck").

# CLICHÉ NO. 34

## RUN LIKE A SCALDED DOG

Those who have short legs can run faster than those with long legs. Have you noticed? I have long legs, and I can't run very fast. Short legged fellows could always beat me, except when I was scared. But, when I get scared, I can do some amazing things that I never dreamed I could do. That's true with most people.

For instance: I read, one time, where a little bitty woman, about the size of Phyllis Diller, picked up the front end of a car, after a wreck, to allow one of her "younguns" to scamper out from under the wrecked car!

Where did her amazing strength come from? They tell me that it came from adrenalin flowing within her.

When you get scared, adrenalin flows. The more scared you get, the more adrenalin will flow. If you get scared enough, your hair will stand up (again, like Phyllis Diller's hair. She must stay scared).

I have been almost that scared. One time, when some boys and I were playing hooky from school, cops almost caught us. We ran, like scalded dogs, and hid in some bushes, and the cops drove by, very, very slowly, but they missed us. I'm sure that my hair was standing up on my arms, legs, and head (I could feel it). I was scared!

Another time I got scared was when I went rabbit hunting with two of my brothers. We each had a gun and we had a couple of hounds with us. Suddenly, one of the dogs had a fit! (Something must have been biting him inside his guts). I had never seen a dog have a fit. The dog ran towards me like a scalded dog, yapping, and barking! I got scared (My hair stood up like Phyllis's hair). I threw up my shot gun and took aim at the dog and BAM!! I missed! The dog kept right on running, past me, and off into the woods.

My older brother scolded me for shooting at the poor dog. He said that the dog was having a fit. And, looking back, I know that my brother was right, because the dog was not barking at anything, not at me, not at a rabbit, not at a 'possum, nothing! But, at the time, I wasn't taking any chances. The adrenalin was flowing in me. I was scared stiff.

Another time that my adrenalin flowed like that: The chief of police, in town, had a grown son whose name was Bruce. He was maybe 21 or 22. He was short and stubby, with bowed legs. He was built for running. But, his butt stuck way out behind him!

Some boys and I, about four of us 12 or 13 years old, were walking down a path, through some woods, and we passed Bruce, who was walking in the opposite direction.

After we passed, I said (out of the corner of my mouth): "Hey Bruce, why don't you stop and let your butt catch up with you?" As soon as I said it, I knew I was in trouble!

He took off after me, and I never ran so fast in my life! I could see him, out of the corner of my eye, reaching for me. If he had caught me, he would have skinned me alive (His butt didn't catch up with him, but he almost caught up with mine).

I zigged and I zagged. When I did, he didn't cut in time, and I left him. He became exasperated and gave up the chase. My buddies died laughing. They thought it was funny! But, it wasn't funny to me. He scared the day lights out of me!

That's one time that I ran like a scalded dog. I was amazed at my self. But, when the adrenalin flows, one can do amazing things.

I had a buddy one time, that told me this story: He had been seeing a beautiful lady. He met her at a dance, a night club, a bar, or somewhere. But, she never told him that she was married. He took her home, kissed her goodnight, and got in his car and left.

A few nights later, he thought he would call on her again. He knocked on her door and this guy came to the door. My buddy said that he thought the guy was her daddy. He was bald headed and he looked old enough to be her daddy. So, my buddy asked him: "Is your daughter home?" The man happened not to be her daddy but her husband! (Can you imagine?)

The man said: "So you're the S.O.B. that's been seeing her! Wait right here!!

My buddy said that he didn't bother to wait, but took off running with his short legs pumping. He was a fast runner anyway, but when the adrenalin started flowing, he could flat fly!

The man came back with his 12 gauge Remington automatic shotgun and BAM! BAM! BAM! But he missed. My buddy had run, like a scalded dog, and hid behind a tree!

# CLICHÉ NO. 35

## CAUGHT WITH HIS BRITCHES DOWN

Caught red handed (I don't know how this cliché got started). Up the creek without a paddle (this one neither). Caught with his britches down (but I believe I know, definitely, how this one got started. My brother, "Dub", started it).

All of the above clichés mean the same thing: "Caught in the act"!

Farmers used to congregate, in Iva, on Saturdays. They came with their mules and wagons, and with their horses and buggies, and in their "T" model Fords.

They tied their mules and horses to hitching posts, or to a tree, or to a lamp post (we did have a few street lights, back then, not many, but a few), and they parked their "T" models anywhere, and everywhere, but mostly, down town, in front of the train depot, and along the side of the road that is now known as Front Street.

There was a well, with a hand pump, and a watering trough, for watering the mules and horses.

Back then, just before the great depression, farmers had plenty of money to spend, and believe me, they would spend it. They were not used to having all that money, and the money burned holes in their pockets!

My "paw", as poor as he was, bought a brand, spankling, dankling, new 1929 "A" model Ford touring car, with a rag top, light grayish green. It was a beautiful car, when it had the top.

He didn't have it but for about three months, when a "no good" cousin of his (there were a lot of "no goods" back then, same as there are today), stole the car, while my "paw" was sleeping off a hang over on the front porch, and went for a joy ride.

The cousin couldn't drive very well (not many people could, back then. They were used to driving mules and wagons, not cars), and "paw's" cousin ended up in a big ditch (there were a lot of deep ditches along sides of the roads) with "paw's" brand, spankling, dankling, new Ford touring car turned upside down! Needless to say, that nice, black, canvas rag top was crushed.

I don't know what "paw" did to his cousin about stealing his car. I do know that "paw" got his car back, minus the top. He never did have the top replaced. I guess the depression had set in and he didn't have enough money. But, "paw" drove that car, like that, without a top, for a long time (talk about the Beverly Hill Billies, but they had nothing on us).

Getting back to all those farmers in town on Saturdays: They would come and spend all day; consequently, they needed to use the bathroom, occasionally. We didn't have places like Burger Kings, Subways, McDonalds, etc., places with public bathrooms. But, Iva did have two outhouses. The outhouses had two holes in each outhouse which could accommodate four farmers at a time.

The outhouses were located down town, behind where the old fire station is today. The outhouses were used by other folks, also, and not just by the farmers. Sometimes, they were used by boys, playing hooky from school. We cotton mill hill boys played hooky a lot, I'm ashamed to admit.

Some of us boys were playing hooky one day, and my brother, "Dub", felt the urge to go use one of those two hole outhouses. After he had gone in, pulled his britches down, closed the door, and got on the seat, I saw someone coming. I could tell by the man's easy, sure- footed gait (like he was plowing a mule) that he was, of all people, my "paw".

We other boys scampered, like ants, behind some bushes, where we could peep, and left poor "Dub" in the outhouse. We thought that "paw" would pass on by, and that "Dub" would be safe.

But "paw" had the urge to go, too. I could tell by the way he picked up the pace, when he got near the outhouse. When he reached the outhouse, he opened the door, and low and behold, he saw "Dub" setting there. Even though there were two holes, one for "Dub" and one for "paw", "paw" decided to wait for "Dub" to get through with his business and come out, before he went in.

And he waited, and he waited, and he waited. "Dub" never did come out. Finally, "paw" opened the door again and there was no "Dub". He had slipped out the other hole that had not been used since the last cleaning. (Just for your information, the outhouses were built with the lower part of the back open and a hired hand would come by, with mule and wagon and a tank and lime, once a week, to clean the outhouses).

Caught with his britches down. That's how that cliché got started! "Dub" started it!

# CLICHÉ NO. 36

## PACKED LIKE SARDINES IN A CAN

Southerners used to have big families. Farm help was scarce, and farmers needed cotton pickers, fodder pullers, corn shuckers, plow hands, hog sloppers, wood cutters, water toters, etc. Tasks that children, boys and girls, could do (There should have been a law against it, but there wasn't. Times were hard back then).

I know that I have told you this before, but I'm going to tell you again: My "paw" and "maw" had ten children, five girls and five boys.

My mama's sister, Aunt Verna, also, had ten children (cousins of mine). My mama had other sisters and brothers that had big families. I'm not going to name them all (I can't), but most of them were farmers, like my dad. I have cousins, galore. I have cousins that I have never seen. Every week, it seems, I run across a new cousin that I didn't know I had.

Well, my sweet little Austrian war bride and I didn't want the big Southern family tradition to die, even though we were not farmers and didn't need children to help us work (my children don't know what work is), we had seven children, three girls and four boys.

I had a lady to ask me, one time: "Where did you all sleep, in that little bitty house"? I said: "We didn't have any problem sleeping. The house had three bedrooms, one for my wife and me, one for the girls, and one for the boys. Some of them had to sleep together, like I had to sleep with my brother, Richard, when I was a boy, but that wasn't bad, we could help keep the bed warm. I guess that's one reason that I always felt real close to my brother, Richard. I got to know him real good.

The problem with the little bitty house was not the sleeping arrangements. The problem was with the bathroom. We had only one. And that was a problem, especially when someone had to go real bad, and someone else had beat them to the bathroom. And that happened frequently, almost everyday.

You should have seen our house, in the mornings, when kids were getting ready to go to school. We had to put a five minutes limit for anyone using the bathroom. At other times, one could stay a little longer.

I remember, one time, my son, George, when he was just a little boy, asked my wife; "Mama, can I use the bathroom?" That might sound like a silly question, but at our house, that was a good question.

Our bathroom was not the only place that was crowded. Our '55 Chevrolet, blue and white, station wagon was crowded, too. (Especially, on Sundays when we were all going to church).

Normally, I called the roll to be sure that all the kids were in the car, before taking off. But, one Sunday, after church, I goofed.

We had gotten home, and changed clothes, when the telephone rang. I answered the phone, and I heard the voice of a little girl about eight or nine years old say: "Daddy, you left me!" We had left my darling little daughter, Maggie. I had to rush back down there (3 or 4 miles) to get her.

We were like Old Mother Hubbard who lived in a shoe. We had so many children that we didn't know what to do!

One day, in the hot summer,, we decided to take the kids to McDonalds to give them a treat. The 55 Chevrolet station wagon didn't have air conditioning. Before we got to McDonalds, all the kids were shouting out their orders: "I want a Big Mack. I want a double decker. I want Mac Nuggets. I want this and I want that. My little son, George, who was about five, sitting squashed up in the middle of the back seat, said: "I want some air!"

Packed like sardines in a can, that's what my kids were in that '55, blue and white, Chevrolet station wagon, that day!

# CLICHÉ NO. 37

## NOT A DROP IN THE BUCKET

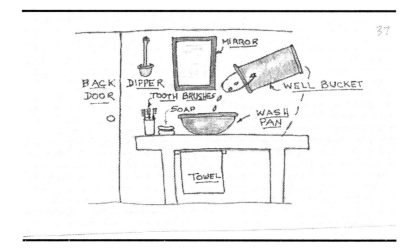

Our well was deep. It must have been at least fifty feet deep. That's a long ways down, when you have to draw water, one bucket at a time. That's a long ways down, especially, for young boys to have to draw enough water to water four sweaty, thirsty mules that have been pulling a plow, in the hot sun, from sun-up 'til noon, or from one-thirty 'til dark. We had to give the mules water twice a day. You could lead those mules to water, but you didn't have to worry about making them drink. They were always thirsty, and every time we watered them, they drank gallons.

Our well bucket held two gallons. We had to let that bucket down and draw it back up at least twice for each mule. That's eight times, every time we watered the mules. That's a lot of turning that winch, and catching that bucket when it got to the top, and pouring the water in tin tubs for the mules to drink.

But that's not all. We had to draw water for our cow and her calf. It takes gallons of water to make milk. And we drank lots of milk, and ate lots of cornbread, at our house. Our cow was a Jersey, and she gave lots of creamy milk (that's why I have such good teeth). But, in order to produce that milk, my brothers and I took turns at drawing water for our cow. We had to be sure that she didn't go thirsty, like our mules did sometimes. Her watering trough was not allowed to run dry. We kept water in her trough all the time. If she got thirsty, she could just amble over there to her trough and take a sip.

And that's not all; our chickens had to have water, also. Every time that we drew water, whether it was for the cow, or mules, or for something else, we had to fill up the watering pan for the chickens.

In addition, our hogs had to have water. The hogs, not only drank lots of water, mixed in with their slop, but they had to have water for a wallowing hole, in the shade. Hogs get hot and lose fat, if you don't keep them cool. If they were to become fat and sassy, and hoggish, and produce lots of ham, bacon, and sausage, we had to keep them happy, and it took lots of water.

Our household demanded lots of water for drinking, making tea, cooking, washing our faces, and for washing our dirty clothes. It's a good thing that our well was deep, with a good stream. Some folks' wells would dry up in the hot summer time, when there was a long dry spell, but ours never did run dry. (And, some folks wouldn't get a drop in the bucket, when they went to draw water. What a shame!)

People today don't know how lucky they are. They can just turn on a faucet and get all the water they want. And, today, there are bathrooms in the house, and we don't have to go outside, in the cold winter, to use the bathroom.

When people first got running water in their homes and put bathrooms in homes, there was an old farmer who said: "They're crazy. I'll never have a toilet in my house!"

We have come a long way, baby, since I was a little ole barefooted country boy.

Believe me, it was a chore for me and for my brothers to draw all that water, in order to keep anything, and every thing from going thirsty.

We kept our drinking water in a bucket, on a table in the kitchen, near the back door. There was a dipper, hanging on a nail above the bucket. Every time, it seemed, that I went to get a drink of water, the bucket would be empty. There would not be a drop in the bucket, and off to the well I would go to draw another bucket of water.

That was the good old days. That's what some folks say. But, I'm glad that I have, finally, got running water in my house!

# CLICHÉ NO. 38

## WEASEL OUT OF IT

A weasel is a long, skinny, sneaky animal. A weasel has a long neck, a long tail, little short legs (but it can run fast), and has a long nose (which is used for nosing, and poking around), and big pop eyes.

A weasel is first cousin to the animal that has a white stripe down its back, a skunk. There are lots of skunks around here, but I don't recall ever seeing a weasel (I guess they are around, but they can sneak and hide so well that we just don't get to see them).

I know they were around our country home, when I was growing up, for we had a lot of hen eggs missing, from time to time. "Paw" said: "It must be weasels that are stealing our eggs."

Farmers have a lot of trouble with weasels. They get in chicken houses, at night, and not only steal eggs, but they steal baby chicks, pullets, hens, and maybe every once in a while, they will steal a red rooster.

A farmer wakes up, hears his chickens squawking, and by they time he gets his gun and runs to the chicken house, the weasel is long gone, through a crack, and is out in the barn, bothering the mules. I know that it must have been weasels that pestered our mules for the mules kicked all the planks off the walls in our barn!

Skunks are, also, pests. They get in people's garbage. When I lived near Starr, one was messing around, outside my bedroom window. I didn't know what it was, so I raised the window to take a look, and the skunk sprayed me good! It took days for that stink to go away.

And another time, I was on a trip with two other fellows with the Federal Aviation Administration surveying for a power line. As we were walking through some woods, we heard something rustling in the leaves. I, and one of the fellows, walked on. But, the other fellow was curious and nosey. He went back to see what was making the noise in the leaves. When he kicked the leaves, (you guessed it) it was a skunk! The skunk sprayed my comrade real good. He really did stink up our car.

Weasels and skunks are bad animals. I would hate to be called either one. They are looters, like a neighbor we had, way back yonder, when we lived on the mill hill. He was famous for getting in people's coal piles. Most people, on the mill hill, heated their homes with coal burning fireplaces. This fellow would even steal coal from us (from our scrawny, measly, little coal pile). Snuffy Smith and weasels had nothing on him. My mama called him a weasel. The police could never catch him. (Come to think of it, he did look like a weasel. But, he had a white stripe down his back like a skunk! He was a theft, and a no good, stinking coward). I wish they would catch them all and lock them up, and throw away the key, and not let them weasel out of it. (Like they seem to always do).

# CLICHÉ NO. 39

## CRIED UNCLE

The south has changed. Back when I was a youth, there were not many college-educated dudes. That's what we called those that were educated: "Dudes". It seemed to me, that it was almost a shame and disgrace to have a good education. The vast majority of Southerners had very little education, and it showed.

If you go further back, you will find that people had less education (The Iron Age).If you go far enough back, you will find that no one had an education.

I'm not an evolutionist. That is, I don't believe that the world and everything that's in it just happened. I believe there is a God in control of everything. But, I firmly believe that there was a time that men lived in caves. They carried big clubs around on their shoulders, and they drug women around by the hair of their heads. (Land of Moo. Alley Oop. There was a time).

I'm glad that the South is not what it used to be. I'm glad that I had a pretty teacher, by the name of "Sue Stribling" (bless her heart), that inspired me to climb out of the gutter (so to speak), and go to college, and become an enjuneer (When I was in her class, I couldn't even spell enjuneer, now I are one! I know that she would be proud of me).

I'm convinced that the reason we have so much turmoil, terrorists, bombings, and killings in the world today is because there are people who still live like Alley Oop in caves (look at Afghanistan), and they have no desire to climb out, and wash themselves up, and to go to school and be somebody!

I think that the best thing that this world could do is for all nations to unite, and combine our efforts, and gather all the animal-like people up the world over, and build a fence around them, and send them to school, with Sue Stribling as their teacher, and teach them to be somebody!

The Deep South, back when I was a country lad, was full of people who never went to school a day in their lives, and there were many undisciplined, unruly, vicious, and mean people.

I was at a ball game between Jackson Mill and Orr Mill, one time, when a fight broke out between my brother-in-law and some fellows from Orr Mill. My brother, Richard, said to me and another brother John: "Let's go and help "ole" Dewey, my brother-in-law." So, we went over to where the fight was going on, and this fellow came running by me, chasing Dewey. I grabbed the guy and threw him to the ground. John put his hand on the guy's face, while he was on the ground, and the fellow had a cigarette in his mouth that stuck up between John's fingers (I can see him now), and John drew back his fist, like he was going to smash him, but he never did. He let the guy up, and an Iva spectator came running up to me and said: "Here, Amos, take this knife, and cut him to pieces." He put a big pocketknife, with a blade of about six inches, in my hand. I gave the knife back to Him. I wasn't about to cut anybody. I wasn't that mean, and ignorant, and stupid. But Iva was full of people who would have cut the man!

We told the guy that we would let him go, but not to hurt our brother-in-law. He said okay. We hung around for a while, and left.

There were a lot of fights back then. Almost every Saturday, somebody would get the "heck" beat out of themself. I think it was due to illiteracy. People were, no doubt, a whole lot more ignorant than they are today. People let their animal nature (their cave man nature) dominate and control their lives.

What was so sad: "I was one of them"! No one could make me say: "I'm sorry"! That was not in my vocabulary. My mama couldn't even make me say I'm sorry, not even with a hickory stick.

One day, my mama and a huge colored lady by the name of "Big Mildred" were washing clothes. I gave my mama some sass, and she grabbed me by my overall's strap and beat the fool out of me with a peach tree sapling. She said: "Say you're sorry!" I said: "No! I will not!" She beat me some more and said, again: "Say you're sorry!" I said: "No! I will not!" I was just a dumb, ignorant, stubborn, Southern country boy. Finally, mama quit beating me and "Big Mildred" said: "If that was my youngun, I would stand him up in the corner and cut him to pieces with my razor!"

Man, I was glad that I was not one of her younguns (for more reasons than one). Had I been one of her younguns, I do believe that I would have said: "I'm Sorry. Lordy, Lordy, I'm sorry!" That would have been a time that I would have cried "Uncle"!!

I'm glad that those days are gone forever. Now days, boys and girls, in the South are going to school. I wish other places in the world like the Mid East, Africa, some places in Asia, would clean up their acts and follow our example and become somebody! Don't you?

# CLICHÉ NO. 40

## MAD AS A HORNET

Hornets, pit bull dogs, and gamecock roosters have a lot in common: They like to fight. I don't know what it is that makes them so mad at everything. It must be in their hormones.

Have you ever looked a pit bull dog in the eyes? He goes around, all day, with a frown on his face. He looks to be mad. His eyes are flaming mad. I don't believe anything could make him smile, like a lot of other good Southern bred dog's smile, with their tongues hanging out.

My brother, Alvin, had a pit bull dog. A stray had puppies at the Greenville-Spartanburg Airport, where my brother worked, and he took one of the puppies home and fed him (with Alpo can dog food that should have made any dog happy), and the dog grew and became an adult; but he was never happy. He was always mad about something.

Alvin had a plow for sale, and he put it out on the front lawn with a "For Sale" sign. A fellow (a total stranger) stopped by to look the plow over. Alvin saw the man out there and went out to "wheel and deal" with him. When suddenly! Like a bolt of lightning, Alvin's pit bull dog came flying out of the barn, and jumped on the man's back, on his shoulders, and tried to bite the man on his neck. Alvin knocked the dog off the man, kicked the dog, scolded him and sent him back to the barn! I don't think the man got bit, but Alvin lost a sale for the man didn't want to hang around and "wheel and deal", after that. He ran, as fast as his legs could carry him and got in his pick-up and left, with his tires screaming. He was in a hurry, and I don't blame him. It's a wonder that he didn't sue Alvin; but he didn't. He was a Southerner and we don't do that down South. (Yet).

Gamecocks are the same as pit bull dogs. They strut around, with their chests stuck out, looking for a fight. If they can't find another rooster to fight, they will fight anything (A cat taking a nap in the hay, a dog smelling around a cow pile, little boys with cotton sacks hanging from their shoulders, country women with clothes baskets under their arms). Gamecocks will fight anything that moves!

Johnny Cash was born to sing Southern Country music. Gamecocks are born to fight. That's their talent (besides crowing a lots).

In the old days, there were a lot of rooster fights, down South. Many people made their living by raising fighting gamecocks. There would be cockfights almost every Saturday. That was a big time sport. People bet money, big money! (I'm talking about five dollars!), on their roosters.

I never attended a cockfight, but my brother did, after the cockfights were outlawed, and he got caught, along with several other good ole Southern boys. The cops confiscated their money and took'em to jail.

There are not many cockfights around anymore. The gamecocks have fizzled out. It doesn't seem that there's a fight left in'em. They have forgotten how to fight.

Look at the score!! Clemson 63 and the Carolina Gamecocks 14! I wouldn't call that a fight. Would you? (Hey! If you happen to be a Gamecock fan, I hope I didn't ruffle your feathers. I know you will be back, and maybe jump on those tigers like a chicken on a

June bug! It may be EONS away, but you will be back. What goes around will come around. They always say).

Hornets, pit bulls, and gamecocks, and there is one other group: "Little bitty women". They have a lot of spunk, and they go around, all day, looking for someone to beat up on.

"Stick" was a good ole Southern boy. He wouldn't hurt a fly. He was always happy. He was always the life of a party. I can hear him, now, fussing at the umpires at Jackson Mill baseball games: "You low down rotten scoundrel, you", he would say, and the crowd would roar. They liked "Stick"!

I guess "Stick" visited every state in the union, riding in a freight train boxcar, as a hobo. Even though he had a bad leg and had to use crutches, he still could hobo those freight trains.

Poor ole "Stick", he would drink anything, if he thought there was alcohol in it, (Rubbing alcohol, bay rum, even white shoe polish strained through loaf bread). He was a sot.

He had never been married. He was about forty five, or so, when a little bitty woman thought she could tame him, and make a husband out of him. She married "Stick".

I couldn't believe it! "Stick" got married! It spread like wild fire all over town! Women talked about it in grocery stores (I should have said: they talked about it in the Dixie Store, for we had only one). Men talked about it in the Mill Barber shop. "Stick's" drinking buddies talked about it in North Iva beer joint.

That fiery little woman, the one like a pit bull dog, or like a gamecock, married "Stick". Poor ole "Stick", his hobo days were over, I thought, and a lot of other people thought. We thought that woman, with the fire in her eyes, would tame him, for sure. But, not so! We underestimated "Stick".

Although the woman was about the meanest woman on earth, she could not tame "Stick"! "Stick" was not to be domesticated.

He did not own a car. He couldn't drive, with his lame leg and all. He had to depend on his little wife to take him places, and she did drive him about, when they first got married.

She would drop him off at North Iva, and let him have a beer or two, and then she would take him home, lock the door, and wouldn't let him go out again until she said so!

"Stick" put up with that for a while, but his heart got to longing for the "good old days", when he could sit around the pot belly stove with his buddies and get "drunk as a skunk" and make them laugh! So, one day, he slipped out of the house, while his little bitty wife, with the fire in her eyes, was gone. And "Stick" made his way, on crutches, to his most favorite spot on earth: "The North Iva Beer Joint"!

She came home and found him gone. I'll show that stinking, lowdown, good for nothing, scoundrel, she said to herself. She got in her car and went straight to North Iva, where she knew she would find him. She came busting in the door, like a category five hurricane (I was there, having a cool one, and I saw it). She grabbed poor ole "Stick" by the right ear (or it might have been his left one), she slapped him on his head (he had his arms up, trying to ward off her blows), and she pulled him, and drug him out the door, mad as a hornet, and shoved him into the car and took him home!

But, like I said, she couldn't tame "Stick". He was back at North Iva time after time, and she would come and pull his ears, punch him, and slap him, and take him home. Finally, she gave up and went back to where she came from. And ole "Stick" was allowed to live out his last days the way he liked: Getting drunk, telling stories, and making people laugh.

Hornets, pit bulldogs, gamecocks, and little bitty women have a lot in common: They stay mad and ready to fight!

# CLICHÉ NO. 41

## TOO BIG FOR HIS BRITCHES

Have you ever watched The Beverly Hill Billies? Are you that old? There was Uncle Jeb, Granny, Jethro, and Ellie Mae. They reminded me of some Southern folks that I know real well: Namely (I hate to say it. Lord, I hate to say it but I have to), the Terry family (my family). I hang my head in embarrassment. But it's true.

"Paw" was like Uncle Jeb in so many ways that it's pitiful. Listen, I'm "paw's" son. He raised me. Even though he fed me beans, fatback, and black molasses, he still raised me. And I know "paw" real well. I know him like the back of my hand. He and Uncle Jeb would pass for brothers. They looked alike, with their floppy hats. They sounded alike, their voices, vocabulary of country (real country) language, and they hopped around alike, especially after drinking white lightning (both liked that stuff).

I realize that with The Beverly Hill Billies that it was Granny who had the recipe, and the one who made the white lightning.

While at our house, It was "paw", and not "maw", that made it (well, "paw" didn't make it in the house. He wouldn't dare). He slipped and made it down in the woods, by the creek in a copper liquor still, that he built himself. I know that he made liquor for he made me help him, one time, only one time. After that time, my conscience bothered me, and I told my mama to speak to "paw". She did, and I didn't ever have to help him make the stuff again. Looking back, I think that he probably was trying to teach me the trade of making "moonshine". That was a trade that a lot of Southerners followed, back then.

"Paw" learned the trade way back yonder, back during the prohibition days. In those days the Federal Government was the only one that was allowed to make liquor. The Government had a still down on the banks of the Savannah River, near where "paw" was born and raised. The still was a big one. The Federal Government employed many workers to run the still. My "paw" and his brothers were employed there. That's where "paw" learned to make liquor (Ain't it a shame, The Federal Government teaching our men such a trade?)

Well, after the government quit making liquor, and allowed others to make it (provided they paid heavy taxes), the workers of the many stills around found themselves unemployed, and liquor making was the only trade they knew.

That's when illegal liquor stills began to pop up all over the South (especially, in hard to get to places, like the mountains). The government wasn't getting any money from the illegal "moonshine", and they didn't like it a bit. So they sent "Revenuers" to track down and capture the "moonshiners", take'em to jail and destroy their liquor stills. The Federal Agents pestered the "moonshiners" so much that they said: "What the heck. I better quit making "moonshine" and find something else to do." And most of'em started hauling pulpwood, except for "paw", he decided to be a cotton farmer (and make a little "moonshine" on the side for his personal consumption).

Yes, "paw" resembled Uncle Jeb in so many ways. When I saw The Beverly Hill Billies on TV for the first time, in their "A" Model Ford Touring car, without a top, I know that my face must have turned red, for I was embarrassed. I knew that folks around Iva would see that show and they would say: "There goes the Terry family"! Our car was just like the Clampet's car.

"Maw" resembled Granny some, too. They dressed alike in long cotton dresses (all ladies wore dresses, back then. Pants weren't allowed for women). But "maw" wasn't skinny and spry like Granny. "Maw" was more laid back and had more flesh. Also, "maw" wasn't nearly as bossy as Granny, except she would nag "paw" when he had been hitting the bottle.

The only difference in our family and that of the Beverly Hill Billies was: We didn't have an Ellie Mae. I wished we did. It would have been a whole lot more fun around our house. My sisters were older. They were pretty, but they didn't have the body and personality of Ellie Mae.

We didn't have an Ellie Mae, but we had a Jethro. Again, I hang my head in shame. I'm embarrassed. Lord, I hate to say it, but the Jethro in our family was, no other than me! Remember how Jethro was always too big for his britches? His coat would just barely button. His pants were too tight, and too short. He was just like me. They called me "Big Butt Amos".

I remember my first suit. "Paw" and "maw" took me to Pennys and bought me a suit when I was fifteen. I looked good in it for about six months. I grew so fast that it soon became too small. But, I continued to wear it. I looked like Jethro, too big for my britches!

# CLICHÉ NO. 42

## SMART AS A WHIP

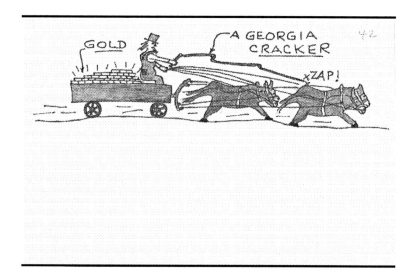

I might get some argument about this, but I have heard that a Georgia Cracker is a whip, and not some poor old Georgia cotton farmer who eats sardines and soda crackers (I've seen some of these, too. One was from Elberton. He, not only, ate the sardines, but he turned up the can and drank the juice! UGH!)

The way that Georgians became known as "Georgia Crackers" was like this: Back during the time when Georgia first became a State, there was gold in "dem dar" hills, up around Dahlonega, and at a place named, of all things, Gold Mine, and at some other places.

The Georgians mined gold and hauled it back to Atlanta to smelt it, refine it, roll it out, and beat it into thin (very, very thin) sheets to use to plate the dome roof of Georgia's State Capital. If you have been to Atlanta, you have seen the gold dome roof of the State Capital. That is how the gold got up there on that roof.

The gold was transported from the mines, in North Georgia, to the State Capital by mule train.

Now, as you know, whenever gold was being transported, anywhere in the old days, there would be thieves and robbers (no good bandits who didn't want to get a job and make a living and be somebody), lying in wait to rob those mule trains, or the steam engine powered trains, or the horse drawn stage coaches that was used to transport that gold.

Well, I'm telling you what's the truth: Those bandits met their matches, when they tried to rob those Georgia Mule Train Drivers!

You have heard, I'm sure, like I have, about the State of Georgia being settled by a fellow with the name "Oglethorpe". Now, Oglethorpe was no "sissy". He was an Englishman, and liked his brown stout and bitters in a mug, like all Englishmen do, but he was tough and a man with a big heart. (As are a lot of his Southern descendents).

And Oglethorpe brought over, on his ship, some folks who had a tough time making ends meet in England. They were poor and destitute. Some of the immigrants were criminals that English judges, with their long black robes and long gray wigs, had pardoned from English jails provided the criminals would get on Oglethorpe's boat and get the "hell" out of England and never come back!

Oglethorpe anchored his boat at Savannah, and his poverty stricken passengers, criminals and all, got off the boat, kissed the ground, and began to disperse in all directions across the state of Georgia.

Some went to Dahlonega, some went to Gold Mine, some went to Clayton, and one went to Elberton (That's the one that I saw drinking the juice from the sardine can. Poor fellow, after all these years, he was still destitute).

Well, I have always heard, and you have probably heard, too, that you can take a boy out of the country, but you can't take the country out of the boy. And, I personally know that this is a true statement. I have been all around this world, several times, and I'm still just a plain old country boy.

The Settlers of Georgia, Oglethorpe's passengers, had known some tough times in England. And they were in for some tough times in Georgia, but they were up to the task. They were "tough cookies", and they were to become "tough Georgia Crackers". All their descendents are like that. All the Georgians that I know, and I know a lot of them for I lived in Georgia for about twenty years, were tough people. (The Georgia Bull Dogs are an example of this toughness).

Well, of those descendents of Oglethorpe, who migrated to various places in Georgia, some became cotton farmers, some became flea market dealers, some became "boot-leggers", and a few became mule train drivers that hauled gold from the mines in the mountains of Georgia back to Atlanta.

The last bunch are the ones that I want to talk about: The mule train drivers. Any "ole" Southern Country boy, that was raised on a farm, will tell you that if you are going to drive a wagon, which is pulled by several mules, that you have to be strong. You have to be strong enough to be able to seesaw the bits in the mules' mouths, and to use a whip to get their attention in order to get them to do what you want them to do. It's quite a chore to get mules to back up to get a load of firewood, or a load of sugar cane, or a load of GOLD! Hey! That's a big chore and one has to be strong and have big muscles.

And another thing: Mule train drivers had to be stubborn. They were dealing with stubborn animals. Mules are the most "mule headed" animals around. Mule train drivers had to be more stubborn than the mules (That's another trait that you can't get out of Southern Country boys, like me).

Finally, mule train drivers, especially if the mule train was long, would have to be a "crack shot" with a whip, a very long whip, long enough to reach the butt of a mule, that may be way up that was not pulling his share of the load, or was balking and acting up and being contrary.

That's where the "cracker" came in. The cracker was a long whip. It may have been as long as twenty feet. (That's a long whip).

The Georgia mule train drivers were crack shots with those crackers, and used them on the butts of their mules hauling gold from the gold mines in North Georgia back to Atlanta. And occasionally, but not very often, the drivers used those crackers on the butts of "no good", lazy, thieving infidels that thought they could robe those mule trains of the gold.

The cracker was a long whip, made of cowhide or rawhide. The cracker was not a soda cracker that some people may think.

The cracker would sting and draw a blister. It would make one (even a mule) pay attention. It would teach (even a jack ass) to pay attention (our teachers, and our "paws" use to sting our butts in the same manner to teach us a lesson and make us smart).

Smart as a whip. You can't get much smarter!

# CLICHÉ NO. 43

## YOU CAN'T GET BLOOD OUT OF A TURNIP

I disagree. You can get blood out of a turnip. Let me tell you why I know:

You hear old timers, like me, talk about the good old days. Well, I'm here to tell you that the good old days were not all that good. There were some things that were good about the good old days. Like, we had more freedom. We could pray, whenever and wherever we wanted to pray: On the streets (and listen to preachers, too), in our schools (with teachers leading the prayers), before ballgames (before the fights broke out), before we went to bed (Lord I lay me down to sleep). We could pray at any time, without any harassment from federal agencies, and believe me: There was a lot of praying going on in those days for times were hard. Another thing that was good about the good old days: There was not much money floating around. Money was scarce. I know that may sound crazy to you, but, in my opinion, that was a good thing!

That was a good thing because families had to stay at home and eat every measly meal together. We didn't have the money to go gallivanting all over the world. If we wanted to go visiting, it would have to be across the street, or within walking distance. Those kinds of visits were the only kinds we could afford. People loved their neighbors, and that, my friends, was a good thing!

Another thing that was good about the good old days was: We didn't have nearly the federal bureaucracy that we have today. We didn't need it. People were able to govern themselves (papas and mamas and school principals, too).

Even though wages were meager in the good old days, the percentage taken home was more. People were able to spend their hard earned money anyway they chose. They did not have to give it (most of it) to the Federal bureaucracy to use to chop away at some more of our freedoms (and believe me, folks, that was a good thing about the good old days)!

But, like I said, there were some things that were not so good about the good old days: One thing that was not good (during the depression) was that little kids (like me) barely had enough to eat, went cold and miserable in the winter time, and Santa Claus never came around to see them (Ain't that a shame? Every kid deserves to have a visit from Santa; but, many cotton mill kids, and cotton farm kids (back in the good old days) didn't even know who Santa Claus was)! Times were hard for little kids. We had, almost, to raise ourselves. Baby sitters had not been invented.

I hardly ever got to see my mama, except on Saturdays and Sundays. She worked in the cotton mill, on the second shift, and we boys were free to roam. It's a wonder that we didn't get in real trouble (Some boys did, but not in my family).

I remember one boy that got in trouble (real trouble, with my "maw"). He was a friend of my brother. He had a very bad reputation, and my mother had spoken to my brother about it, and tried to get my brother to quit hanging out with him. My brother didn't listen.

Then, one day, one of my sisters, who worked in the mill, also, was taking a bath, in a tin tub, in her room. After she had bathed, and dried herself off, and started to put on her clothes, she noticed a little boy lying under her bed. He had been under there all the time that she was bathing, and not only that, but he had stolen some money from my sister, and he would not give it back!

That's when he really got in trouble! My sister went downstairs and said: "Mama, there's a boy in my room that has stolen some money from me and he won't give it back"!

My mama went up the stairs, with a broom in her hands, and threatened to "whack" the boy up side his head with the broom (and she would have done just that) if he didn't fork over the money. Well, the boy knew that mama meant what she said and he coughed up the dough. And mama chased him out of the house, and said: "Don't you ever come back here again", and he wouldn't dare!

Not all was good about the good old days. Money was scarce. Santa didn't come to see a lot of poor little kids, and many people barely had enough to eat.

In fact, food was so scarce that the mill company planted a turnip patch, in the back alley, behind the mill houses. The turnip patch was big, about 100 feet wide by about 500 feet long. The mill workers had free access to the turnip patch. They could go get a mess anytime they wanted to. My mama sent us boys to the turnip patch quite often. (More than I wanted to go. I hated them). Many times, I came home from school, and looked in the pot on the stove, and found nothing but turnips and turnip greens. I did eat a few, to keep from starving, but not many.

I told you that I would tell you how to get blood out of a turnip. It happened to me.

One day, my mama sent my brother "Dub" and me to the turnip patch to get a mess. After pulling up the turnips, we went out behind the house to wash the turnips and peel them, before taking them in the house. You know how boys like to mess around with anything that you give them to do? That's what "Dub" and I did, and I should have known better. You don't mess around with "Dub".

I would hold up a turnip by its root and "Dub" would take a whack at the root with a sharp knife (He was supposed to cut the root off at the bottom of the turnip). But with each whack he was getting closer and closer to my finger. And, idiot me continued to hold the turnips up by the root for him to whack, and, finally it happened! "Dub" whacked the end of my finger off and blood spurted, everywhere.

"Dub" got blood out cf the turnip that day (and that's what he intended to do, when we first started cleaning those turnips)!

# CLICHÉ NO. 44

## IF YOU CAN'T STAND THE HEAT, GET OUT OF THE KITCHEN

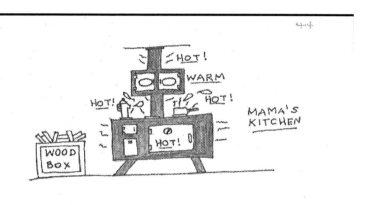

The cooking at our house was done on a big wood- burning stove. The stove had a firebox, and four burners with iron lids that mama would lift off with a lifter which had a spiral ring at the end She would lift the lids off, as needed, so that the black pots that she used for boiling 'taters would be next to the fire. However, she could fry eggs, bacon, flapjacks, apple pies, or what ever on top of the stove (in a black cast iron frying pan) without lifting the burner lids.

The stove had two compartments, with doors, above the cooking surface, through which the stovepipe passed, to keep the food warm, that had already been cooked. These were called "warmers".

The stove had a big oven (it had to be big to hold all the biscuits for our family). The fire, and smoke, passed around the oven then went up through the stovepipe to the chimney. Sometimes, when the wind was blowing hard, back drafts would fill the kitchen with smoke and one had to get out of the kitchen to

145

get some air. Our kitchen stove was big and it generated a lot of heat and smoke, and used a lot of stove wood.

Most of the wood that we used was cut in the fall, after all the cotton had been picked and ginned and sold, and after all the corn had been pulled, shucked, and taken to Burris's Mill (a mill on Wilson's creek with a great big water wheel) to be ground into corn meal, chicken feed, and hog feed. We kept some corn on the cob for the mules.

Cutting the firewood (with axes) in the woods, hauling it to the house, sawing it into firewood lengths (with a crosscut saw), and toting it (in arm loads) into the kitchen, and putting the wood in the wood box beside the stove was chores for us boys. "Paw" did the splitting of the wood.

Like I said, we would cut enough wood in the fall to last all year. We cut pine for the kitchen stove (the pine would produce big flames to go up and lick the cooking vessels, and pine was easier to get a fire started than hardwood). We cut hardwood (oak, sweet gum, hickory, and sometimes, wild cherry) to burn in the fireplace.

We went to the woods, and after we cut down several wagon loads of trees, with an axe (chain saws had not been invented), we would go to the barn and get out the mules and wagon. We would lift the wagon body off and put it aside. We used just the wagon frame for hauling the wood. We could get more logs on the wagon.

After loading the logs, one of us would sit on top, at the front, and drive the mules, and the rest of us would ride the logs hanging off the back end.

We would bring the logs to the house and stack them near an old oak tree, where the mocking birds used to sit and sing to us at midnight, when the moon was shining.

After all the logs had been hauled, and stacked, and after the mules had been put back in the barn, and after the wagon body had been put back on, and after the wagon was safe, under the shed, it was time to start sawing firewood (piles of it).

"Paw" built stands, three of them, shaped like an "X", in which we laid the logs for sawing. We took turns, one on one end of the crosscut, and another on the other end. And we would fuss, and gripe, and pull that saw. "I don't mind you riding, but don't drag your feet." That's what I said to my brother, John. He seemed, to me, to always ride the saw and not do his share of pulling!

Anyway, we would saw up those logs, to firewood lengths, and, then, "paw" would split the logs, with an axe (a very sharp axe). Sometimes, our woodpile would be two stories high and about twenty feet in diameter. It took a lot of wood for our big family.

Sometimes in the summer time (it wasn't so bad in the winter), when mama was cooking, especially, when she was cooking for a Sunday dinner, she had the fire roaring in that big wood stove. Pots were on every burner, and the lids were jumping up and down, and biscuits were in the oven. I'm telling you: "That kitchen got hot"! (Sho 'nough hot!) Mama would open every window, even if the flies did get in, and we had lots of'em from the barnyard, and she would open the back door and stand there for a minute and fan her face with her hands, and wipe the sweat, with her apron (I know what she meant when she complained about bending over that hot stove). Mama's kitchen was hot!

"Paw" liked for his chicken to be fried brown and his cat fish, too. And he liked for his corn pone to have a thick brown crust. It took a hot fire. "Maw" was a good cook, and knew that the way to man's heart was through his stomach. She tried to please her man, and she wanted to please her younguns, too. Most country mamas did.

Harry Truman, our former president, must have been raised on a farm like that in Missouri. And he must have had a mama, like mine, who cooked on a wood burning stove. And his mama's kitchen must have gotten hot (like my mama's kitchen).

He's the one who made this cliché famous, when he said to one of his adversaries: "If you can't stand the heat, get out of the kitchen"! He had experienced a hot kitchen, I'm sure.

But, "Give'em Hell Harry" couldn't stand the heat, himself, when a music critic criticized his daughter Margaret Truman's singing, Harry threatened to punch the critic in the nose!

And do you know what? I agreed with the critic. Margaret's music wasn't country enough for me.

147

# CLICHÉ NO. 45

## HECKLING IS PART OF THE GAME

My "paw" in law and "Stick" Peace were the biggest hecklers that my hometown, Iva, S.C., ever had. Fans used to go to Jackson Mill's baseball games just to hear these two heckle the umpires and the opposing team. And most of the fans joined in the heckling (even me). But, most of the umpires, that I have ever seen, need to be heckled (Where do they get all those blind umpires, anyway)?

Most umpires, that I have ever seen, don't look like they ever played a game in their lives (I'm talking about baseball umpires, here). They are so fat that they just waddle when they walk, and they can't bend over to see whether a baseball is too low or not. They are blind and in need of very thick eyeglasses. They can't tell if a baseball is on the inside, outside, or over the plate. So, they just guess. And half the time their guesses are wrong, just like half my guesses were wrong on Mr. Tiedieman's true-false chemistry tests.

Umpires need to be heckled, and need sand kicked over their shoes, and need tobacco juice spit at their feet, even though it doesn't do any good, but it livens up a dull game.

And opposing team members need to be heckled, too. I know that it's impolite to treat visitors with disrespect. When they come to your house, you ought to give them the best chair, even if it's your favorite rocker by the fire, and you ought to get out your best china to serve them, etc; but, if the visitors are members of an opposing team, that's a horse of a different color. You can forget the politeness. They are fair game for heckling!

Opposing team members need to be heckled. The home team needs all the help they can get, with the fat, blind, and inept umpires and all. Heckling is a big part of the home field advantage.

And besides that: Heckling is fun. It's a great competition to see who can come up with the best heckle of the day. My hat's off to old "Stick" Peace. He came up with a good one, when he said to an umpire: "You low down, rotten scoundrel, you!" Judging by the roar of the crowd, they enjoyed that one. And my "paw" in law had a good one, too, when he said to an opposing team catcher, who was having trouble retrieving a wild pitch: "Why don't you get a stick and kill it!" And again my "paw" in law said about an opposing team's batter: "He's just fat. He can't hit!"

Heckling is part of the game. Little league baseball games wouldn't be half the fun, if parents would keep their traps shut, and not heckle the umps.

Heckling at football games is fun, too. I remember, one time, at a Clemson/Carolina football game, when Clemson fans carried a live rooster out onto the football field at half time, and held the rooster up for the crowd to see, and started plucking his feathers. That was a very good heckle. The Clemson fans loved it! They roared! But, the South Carolina fans didn't think it was all that funny. They swarmed down onto the field to rescue that rooster from his tormentors.

At another Clemson/Carolina game the shoe was on the other foot. South Carolina fans pulled the heckle of the day. Before the game started, a bunch of Carolina fans came out on the field, dressed in Clemson uniforms. When the Clemson fans saw them run onto the field, they let out a roaring welcome. But soon, very soon, the Clemson fans grew silent. A hush came upon them. What was happening? This can't be our "Fighting Tigers"! The Carolina fans, dressed like tiger football players, began to do a ballet dance. It was time for the Clemson fans to swarm the field and express their feelings for being made to look like fools.

149

Yes, heckling is part of the game. Games are more fun when fans join in the heckling. I hope that game officials will be sports and realize this, and don't be like an ump at a ballgame one time who had all he could take from my "paw" in law. He threatened to get the police and put my "paw' in law in jail! Now, that's what I call being a poor sport!

Umpires, and players, too, have no business in the game, if they can't take a little heckling.

# CLICHÉ NO. 46

## HOT UNDER THE COLLAR

Jobs for women were real tough, back in the old days. And so were the jobs for men. And so were the jobs for little boys and girls: hoeing cotton, picking cotton, slopping hogs, milking cows and getting up before sun up to get to work. Oh! My aching back! (I'm familiar with that cliché, because I started it)!

Washing and ironing clothes was no easy task for the women folks, especially for the women folks with large southern families. There were a lot of clothes to wash, and the clothes were dirty, very, very dirty! Folks believed in getting their clothes dirty, back then. Most people would wear their clothes for five straight days without changing them (socks and underwear, too, if they wore any), before the clothes were washed. They would usually take a bath, in a tin tub, on Saturdays, and put on clean clothes, before hitching the mules to a wagon, or before hitching horses to a buggy, and going to town to get a week's supply of groceries.

On Sundays, people would really get dressed up for church. Mama would put on her finest, starting with long silk undies that reached almost to her knees, and then she put on a silk slip, with lace at the bottom. She would always ask me, or someone, if her slip showed. She was very fussy about not wanting her slip to show. But, all women were not that way. One could see quite a few women whose slips showed. But, it looks like mama would have wanted for her slip to show, with all that pretty lace at the bottom. It looks to me like mama would have wanted other women to see what a fine slip she had on.

I think I'm right about this, it's been a long time, but before she put her slip on she put on her corset (She might have put her corset on after the slip. That's how much I know about women's clothes). The corset that she wore was the laced up type, and it had to be pulled really tight, so tight that she had a hard time getting her breath. I've seen her really puff in that thing. The corset had to be tight to please mama. She wanted to have an hourglass figure.

Her Sunday dress was made of silk, also (Ladies wore a lot of silk. Nylon had not been invented). Her dress had long sleeves with lace and ruffles at the cuffs.

Her shoes were black leather with laces, and the shoes came up above her ankles. The heels were about one inch square and about two inches high.

Her hose were made of brown silk (always brown), with a seam at the back. She used a piece of rubber inner tube (but sometimes, she used a fancy garter) above her knees to keep her hose up. She had a time keeping her seam straight. Other women did, too. And, sometimes, her hose would stretch and look all wrinkled and baggy, and she would look real countrified.

"Paw" was a sight for sore eyes when he was dressed in his Sunday clothes. I guess he took a bath. But, like I said before, I don't know if he did or not. After he shaved, with a straight razor, using a brush and soap in a cup, he would put on his BVDs. The BVDs were a sleeveless garment. He did wear underwear, by the way, at least on Sundays. The BVDs straps came over his shoulders. The armpits were open. The legs of the garment came down to his knees. The front had buttons and the seat had a button down flap, in case he felt the urge to go use the outhouse, at home or at church. Both places had outhouses.

After "paw" had put on his BVDs, he sat down and put on his, over the calf, black silk socks (He wore socks on Sunday). He kept his socks up with a garter. The garter looped around behind his knee and back to the front of his legs to a clip that fit over a nodule holding his socks. "Paw" didn't have as much trouble keeping his socks up as "maw" did in keeping her hose up. "Maw" had a problem. That was before garter belts and panty hose.

"Paw" had two dress shirts, a white one, and a blue and white stripped one. But neither shirt had a collar. He used a white plastic, removable collar for either shirt. "Maw" would wash and iron the shirts, but I don't believe she washed the collar. The collar was very stiff, and not suitable for washing. After the collar turned brown at the top, "paw" would throw it away and buy a new collar.

After putting on his dress shirt, "Paw" would put on his black string necktie, which he tied in a bow. Then, he would put a garter on each sleeve of his shirt, above his elbows, and puff out his sleeves. That was the style, back then, for country gentlemen. They thought the garters made them look good.

Then "paw" would put on his blue serge suit. He had only one suit. The suit had a vest with watch pockets. "Paw" always had a pocket watch with a heavy silver chain that sagged down across his chest.

He wore a belt and suspenders to hold up his pants. Southern gentlemen didn't want to be caught with their britches down.

"Paw's" suit coat had narrow lapels with four buttons. He didn't keep his coat buttoned, though, because he wanted folks to see his watch chain.

He wore black leather shoes with rubber soles, and with thick rubber heels.

After church, "paw" couldn't wait to get home and take off his coat and get out of that stiff (very stiff) plastic collar.

And "maw" couldn't wait to get home and get out of that tight (very tight) laced up corset. Many times, I have heard her breathe sighs of relief, after shedding that tight corset.

Plastic shirt collars and laced up corsets are no fun. I'm glad that they have invented button down collars, and I don't mind if they do get floppy. They still look neat, and they don't generate as much heat as the plastic collars.

And I know, that I know, women folks are glad that laced up corsets are not in style anymore. They just let it all hang out, now. It's a whole lot more comfortable.

Hot under the collar (A plastic collar), and hot under the corset (A laced up corset) are things of the past.

Southern ladies and southern gentlemen are happy that they don't have to wear those things, anymore!

# CLICHÉ NO. 47

## LIKE A FISH OUT OF WATER

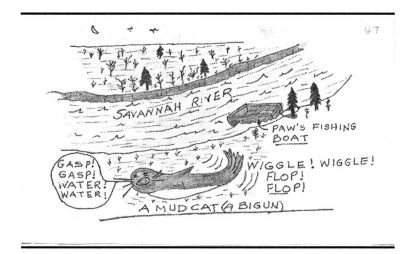

"Paw" was raised on the banks of the Savannah River, way back yonder, when they didn't even have a bridge across the river between Elberton, Georgia and Iva, South Carolina. In order to get across the river, back then, one had to take a ferry: Sander's Ferry, and I understand that my great grand "paw" ran a ferry, later on: Craft's ferry.

Back then, the river had a boats' slew. Boats could travel all the way from Augusta, Georgia (or farther) up to Anderson, S.C. (or farther).

The boats' slew was swift, with mighty rushing currents. I know that it was swift for my "paw" would put all of us younguns in a bateau and push the bateau up and down that river. It's a wonder that he didn't get that bateau cross wise in that slew, and spill all of his younguns; but he didn't. He knew how to push that bateau, with nothing but a very long, slender pole.

After "paw" sold his farm, which was near the river, we moved to the mill hill at Calhoun falls. And later, we moved to Jackson Mill in Iva. "Paw" would still go back to that river every chance he got. He would put fish baskets in the river, and catch catfish.

Sometimes, he would be up 'til midnight cooking fish bait, on "maw's" wood burning kitchen stove, getting ready to go put his basket in the river the next day. I don't know what all he put in that fish bait, but I think he used cottonseed meal and onions. The fish bait sure did smell good, when he was cooking it, and the catfish loved it.

"Paw" really knew how to catch catfish. He knew the best holes to locate his baskets, and places where moochers couldn't find. I don't know how he kept track of the places his baskets were located. There were no floats to mark the spots; but he knew.

And like I said, he would put his younguns in the bateau and go upstream (always, it seemed, upstream) to the places where his baskets were located. He had a steel hook on one end of the pole, and when he got to where he thought he had a basket, he would turn the pole over and start dragging the bottom with the hook. He would snag the steel wire that held his basket and pull the wire up to the boat. Then, he would pull the basket up. And believe me, I'm telling the truth, sometimes that basket would be crammed full, smack full, with catfish (I mean packed). You couldn't get another fish in the basket, if you tried. I'm sure that there must have been other fish, swimming around that basket, and wanting to get inside, but there was no room. Those catfish sure did like "paw's" homemade fish biscuits.

We used to have some good fish fries down there on the banks of the Savannah, and eat watermelon and camp out.

Later, we moved from the mill hill to a farm that was further away from the river, and "paw" had to give up his fishing. I know that he felt like a fish out of water. Fishing for catfish with baskets was a part of him, like his breathing.

It's hard to give up anything that's in your blood. Like it's hard for a country farm boy to leave the country and go live in a city. And hard for a country boy to leave the country and go enlist in the army (Believe me, that's hard). You can take the boy out of the country, but you can't take the country out of the boy. That's a fact of life.

Let me give you an example of what I'm talking about: After the Korean war, some of our politicians from Washington, went over to South Korea to review the troops, and to snoop and try to find something that they could use to make political hay, something that they could blow up, and make headlines in the news. While reviewing the troops, one senator asked a Southern country soldier how did he like the service, was he comfortable, how was the chow, etc. The boy replied that everything was okay, but he sure was homesick, and that he sure did miss his grits. Grits? What are grits? The senator wanted to know (He must have been a Yankee, for Yankees don't know about grits, and buttermilk, and turnip greens, and Southern stuff). The soldier explained to the senator (as best he could in Southern language) what grits were.

Well, the senator went back to Washington and he made a call to the Pentagon and asked to speak to the top general there. He said: "General, I am senator so and so, and I want to know one thing! Why are the soldiers from the South, serving our country in South Korea, not getting their grits?" The general paused and you could hear his brain wheels turning. Finally, he said: "Uh, Uh, Uh, Oh sir, what are grits?" The senator explained to the general (as best he could, with his Yankee knowledge) what grits were. The general understood, and said to the senator: "I will see to it, right away, that all Southern soldiers, wherever they may be stationed, will get their grits served Southern style. Hallelujah, the South has risen again. We have conquered the Yankees this time.

Southerners without grits are like fish out of the water!

# CLICHÉ NO. 48

## STARTED FROM SCRATCH

Chickens and birds have to scratch in the leaves and sand to make a living. I know that on our farm that's what the chickens had to do to find something to eat; but they found plenty: Out in the barnyard. Out in the corn patch. Out in the garden. And out in other places. We hardly ever fed them.

At our farm, chickens had to scratch to make a living. When a hen decided that it was time to quit courting, and flirting with the red roosters, and time to start raising a family, she would find the nest that she liked and start setting on eggs. The nests were nailed to the side of the barn, and we put boards from the ground up to the nests with cross board slats nailed to the boards. That made it convenient for the hens to walk up to the nests, so they could get up there and lay us some eggs to go with the country ham, grits, and homemade biscuits for our breakfasts.

When we noticed that a hen had been setting on a nest for a day or two, and didn't get off, we knew that it was time to put some eggs under her so that her setting would not be for naught.

Mama would pick out about twelve eggs (sometimes fourteen, if the hen was a big dominique) for the hen to set on. The eggs had to be perfect before mama would select them (no double yolkers were allowed). Mama would mark the eggs with a pencil. The reason for marking the eggs was so that we could tell the fresh eggs from the setting eggs, in case another hen got in the nest with our setting hen and laid an egg. We had lots of that going on around our farm (two hens at a time on the same nest).

A setting hen would get off her nest, on occasion, and would run around and squawk, and get herself a drink of water and a bite to eat (That's the time we would feed her a bite, if we heard her squawking), and we would look in her nest to see if there were any fresh eggs.

After about three weeks (you country boys correct me if I'm wrong. I've been out of the country, for a while, but I believe that's right), the hen would get off the nest with her brood of baby chicks. If you have never lived in the country, you don't know what you have been missing. A mother hen with her baby chicks, running here and there, after the mother hen is a beautiful sight.

On our farm, we might have four or five hens, at a time, with baby chicks running around.

We would feed the chicks, once a day, in the evening, with scratch feed (that's cracked corn with wheat mixed in). When we threw the chicken feed out, the mother hens would start calling their chicks, some chicks would be under the house, some out in the bushes in the shade, and some would be out in the barn, but all would hear their mama hens clucking for them, and they would come running, and some that had began to sprout wings would be trying to fly.

Even though there was scratch chicken feed laying all over the ground, the hens thought that they had to scratch to find it, and they would scratch, and they would peck, and cluck, and show their chicks how to eat the feed by pecking up pieces and dropping them back to the ground for the chicks to learn the technique of scratching, pecking, and eating.

The chicks learned how to feed themselves in a hurry, and it didn't take them long to grow into frying size. Frying size was about half grown. And just about every Sunday, mama would tell us boys to go out and catch a frying size for our Sunday dinner (that's our noon meal in case you are a Yankee).

We would kill the roosters, first, before we killed the pullets. We saved all the pullets that we could that they may grow into hens, so that we could get enough eggs to feed our hungry country family.

Like I said: Our chickens had to make most of their own living (They didn't get many hand outs from us). Consequently, they had to do a lot of scratching (What a way to make a living)!

But do you know what? That's the way Southerners had to do, after the Civil War. That had to scratch to make a living.

Times were hard (unbelievably hard) after the Civil War. There were "Carpetbaggers" and "Scalawags", everywhere, stealing, and pilfering, and mooching off of the poor Southerners. (Talking about scam artists: Present day scam artists are no comparison to the "Carpetbaggers" and "Scalawags". These varmints would take food out of the mouths of their own babies, and steal from their own dear mamas that raised them)!

During the war, Yankees came through the South and burned our houses, scorched the very earth, plundered and stole everything that wasn't tied down, even our mules and cows, and left the South desolate (I'm not advocating another Civil War, and I'm not telling you that we should hate the Yankees. I'm just stating a fact). I'm a peace loving, God fearing, Southern gentleman, and we Southern gentlemen would rather make love, and not war!

Shortly after the Civil War, the South began to recover, and people started to make a decent living again. Then bingo! The great depression hit! I was a wee little boy, but I still remember the hard times. Many people died from epidemics. People were frail and weak and starved and unable to cope with things like: Pneumonia, flu, typhoid fever, polio, etc.

The South has been through some hard times, some trying times. Yet, I'm very proud to call myself a Southerner. Southerners have character. Southerners have backbone. Southerners have faith. We have passed many tests.

I know what I'm talking about. Look around. Look at us now. We are on the march. The South is booming. Yankees love to come here to retire!

There's no place like Dixie Land! OH! To live and die in Dixie. The South is the garden spot of the whole world.

And just think! "It all started from scratch!"

# CLICHÉ NO. 49

## THE CREAM OF THE CROP

In the winter time, mama kept her churn by the fire to keep the milk warm. If the milk got cold, the cream would not rise. If the cream did not rise, the milk would not clabber. If the milk did not clabber, she could not churn it. If she could not churn it, we would not have any butter to go with her homemade biscuits. If we did not have any homemade buttered biscuits, we could not eat. We had to have homemade buttered biscuits, at every meal, three times a day, in order to get enough energy to farm from sun up 'til sun down.

Our cow was a Jersey that gave lots of rich, creamy milk that mama made into lots of butter (And don't tell me that butter will hurt you). If you work like we had to work, butter won't hurt you! Red-eyed gravy won't hurt you! Farm raised eggs won't hurt you (Not even double yolker eggs)!

If these things would hurt you, farmers all over the South would have died at an early age; but I know many who are as old as Methuselah! The secret is: Work, work, work, from sun up 'til sun down! That's the way to stay healthy.

Now, if you don't want to work, if you just want to sit around and watch TV, all day long, if you want to let somebody else do all the work and give you handouts, then, these things will hurt you! You will get too lazy to work. You will get fat, like a hog. You will get dependent on others, like a pet cat. You will develop all kinds of health problems like: heart trouble, emphysema, diabetes, etc., and you will gripe and complain that you are not getting enough handouts from working people to satisfy all your cravings!

Lazy lay abouts are like the milk in which the cream won't rise, milk that sours and will not clabber. This kind of milk is not fit to make butter. It is not fit to drink with mama's cornbread, that has a yummy brown crust, even the hogs won't slurp it (and hogs will slurp most anything)!

So my message to all lazy lay abouts is to get off your butts and get a job and go to work. Quit your gripping, and quit your complaining. Quit trying to get something for nothing, and start earning your way in life. Work has never hurt anyone! You will feel better about yourself. People will like you better, and will respect you, and you will wake up, and find that you don't have nearly as many problems as you thought you had!

People who are willing to work, those who do over and above that which is required (things not even spelled out in black and white in their job descriptions) are the ones who get the promotions. They are the cream that rises to the top.

Army recruits who obey every command, who keep their shoes shined, shirts buttoned, lockers clean and neat, bunks made, and salute every officer and say "yes sir and no sir" and do everything on the double are the ones who will get the stripes and be made sergeants.

Athletes that exert themselves and practice, practice, practice, until they get all their muscles sore, and get everything down pat and quit making so many stupid mistakes, and who outshine their opponents are the ones who make the megabucks.

I could go on and on: Students who make the best grades, preachers who preach the best sermons, cafes who serve the best Southern style cooking are the ones who are willing to go the extra mile are the cream of the crop.

All of you out there, exert yourself in whatever your hands find to do. Go the extra mile. Become the cream of the crop. You will find that life will be a whole lot more fun!

# CLICHÉ NO. 50

## HE'S A CLUMSY OX

Some people are gifted. Some are dumb. Some are born with intelligence in their genes. I use to think that I had a lot of those genes, until I joined the army. I learned, in a hurry, that I wasn't as smart as I thought I was. I enlisted in the Army (that ought to have shown me, right then, that I wasn't very bright), and I soon learned that plenty people are as smart as me (Well, maybe not all that many; but a few).

Some people are born to be athletes (how lucky can you get)? I didn't have very many athletic genes. I had some, but not many. I played three sports at dear old Iva high, but I wasn't a star in any of them. I could tell that I wasn't a star because the girls didn't flock all around me and try to kiss me, like I see them doing other athletes. They even flock around fat sumo wrestlers who wear nothing but a "G" string. I never could understand females, anyway. It must not be in my genes. I never was much good at sweet-talk either. That's another thing that is not in my genes.

Some people are born with sweet personalities. They come in this world with a smile on their faces. They are happy, outgoing, talkative, never meet a stranger, a pleasure to be around, with more friends than you can shake a stick at. I could do with some of those genes, too. I wish I had them, but they passed me by. I'm the silent type.

There are other genes that I'm glad that I don't have, like lame brain genes. Some people are born as lame brains. They don't know it, but that's what they are. I don't think I have many of those genes (If I do, I don't know it).

These people, with the lame brain genes, are the ones, while sitting in their cars at red lights, waiting for the light to change, are looking in their purses, or talking to their passengers, or looking out the window, and the light has been green for at least five seconds, before they decide to move on (Lame brains! That's what I call them)! I'm glad that I don't have those genes.

I have the other kind: The impatient genes. Maybe you would call it something else, like idiot genes.

Lame brains and Impatients are of opposite genes. Don't try to mix them. It won't work. Both will go crazy.

When I have an appointment, I have to be early. It would kill me to be late for an appointment. And when it's over, it's over, and I'm ready to leave. I don't hang around.

I find that there are not very many people with impatient genes. I'm unique. Almost everybody have the other kind: "The lame brain genes". I know this because everybody else are always getting in my way and won't let me through.

Then there are people with "fat genes". (I feel sorry for them). They are born hungry, and they never get enough to eat. Everything they see reminds them of food. If they are having a conversation about a ball game, for instance, they will sneak in something like, "Oh by the way, did you try their concession stands?"

Another thing about fat people, have you noticed that they congregate together? They love each other's company. Same way that fishermen like to be around other fishermen and tell fish stories', or like country dudes enjoy getting together with other country dudes and talk about the good old days; or like women (country women) congregate in kitchens (at family reunions) and their husbands congregate out in the barn.

Birds of a feather flock together. It's in their genes.

There are other types of genes: "Good looking genes" (I like those genes). Swedish girls and Norwegians have those genes. They have blond genes. I wish all girls, all over the world, would have those genes. What a beautiful world it would be!

Then there are ugly genes, big nose genes, bald head genes, tall genes, runt genes, red hair genes, freckle genes, hairy chest genes, and on and on from one generation to the next.

I had a brother that had "clumsy ox" genes. He didn't know it, but that's what he had. I was his brother, but those genes passed me by (I think).

He had two left feet. When he was little, he was always putting his shoes on the wrong foot. (And he would always forget to tie his shoes).

He tried to play football for dear old Iva High, but he didn't have the genes for football. His "clumsy ox" genes almost got him killed.

Another time his "clumsy ox" genes almost got him killed was when he fell out of the barn loft onto my back. He was handing down kittens from the loft to me and I was putting them in a box. When he fell out of the loft onto my back, I thought seriously about killing him, but then I thought: "The clumsy ox couldn't help it. It was in his genes. So I let him go.

# CLICHÉ NO. 51

## A BALD FACE LIAR

There used to be traveling salesmen, down South, in the old days. I'm sure, if you are old enough, you have heard many jokes about these traveling salesmen. The jokes have just about played out for there are not nearly as many traveling salesmen, today. We have gone to selling things by telecom, by the internet, by TV ads, etc., and traveling salesmen have just about played out (Oh, every once in a while, there might be an encyclopedia salesman, or a group of college students selling vacuum cleaners, stop by). Traveling salesmen jokes have just about become a thing of the past.

But in the old days, there were many traveling salesmen (I've heard my mama talking about them). These salesmen would go out, all over the South, in their horse and buggies. They sold everything, from Rosebud salve to pots and pans (Hey! And let's not forget: silk stockings for the ladies).

And it's true: Farmers would put these salesmen up for the night, and feed them breakfast, and send them on their way the next morning. I remember mama talking about some of these salesmen staying at Grandpa's house, when she was a little girl (Hey, don't you jump to conclusions. My Grandpa did not allow any of those salesmen to sleep with my maw. That joke, about the salesman sleeping with a country girl was about some other country girl and not my maw. So get that idea out of your head, right now)!

People were a lot more neighborly back in those days than they are now. I guess that's a reason we call those days the good old days. There's not much of that neighborliness left, anymore. My Grandpa was one of those good neighbors (He had to be to put up strangers for the night, and traveling salesmen, with their bad reputations, at that)!

I didn't get to know my grandpa all that good. I was still young when he died. My grandma died when I was just a baby. So I didn't know her at all; but I guess she was still living when those traveling salesmen stopped by. Someone had to do the cooking for those salesmen. I'm sure it wasn't grandpa. About all we Southern men know how to cook is catfish and turtle stew on the banks of some stream.

Salesmen like to do business with honest people for they are easy to cheat. And I know that my grandpa must have been a naïve, honest person for a lot of traveling salesmen used to stop by his house.

There was a horse trader in Iva that never sold a bad horse. To hear him tell it: "By granny they were good ones." Salesmen, horse traders, and politicians are all alike: They stretch the truth.

Another one that stretched the truth was my brother. John, when he was showing Paw how many peanuts he got for a nickel, there was a cigarette butt with the peanuts. He said: "Amos must have put that in there." A bald face liar, that's what he was.

# CLICHÉ NO. 52

## TIGHT AS DICK'S HAT BAND

A few years back, not that long ago, when I was a youth, just about everybody wore hats. Men wore felt hats. Women wore a hat that looked like an army helmet to church on Sundays. Boys wore caps that looked like aviator caps with gargles. That was the styles back then.

Southern gentlemen were very polite to women folks. They would hold doors open for them. They would walk on the outside, towards the road. I guess that was to protect the women folks in case a mule and wagon jumped the curb. I'm just joking. There were no curbs, since there were no sidewalks, only dirt roads, mostly. And men would tip their hats to all women that they met, even to strange women that they had never seen before in their lives.

I always felt that the men were flirting, and if the truth is known, I bet they were; but all those Southern gentlemen tipped their hats to women. That was the gentlemanly thing to do. And I noticed that the women would nod back to the men (They seemed to get a kick out of the men tipping their hats to them).

Now, if I had been a man, back then, instead of just a mill hill boy (and know what I know now), when I tipped my hat to a beautiful Southern Belle, and if she nodded back to me, I would have said: "Hey, Honey Babe let's you and me go uptown to Mister Burton's ice cream parlor and have a nickel cone of strawberry ice cream." Or, I might have said: "Honey Doll (that's what I call pretty girls), let's go downtown to the Old Iva Drug Store and sit on a stool by the soda fountain, and sip cider through a straw." Or I might have said: "Let's you get a line and I'll get a pole and we'll go down to the crawdad hole, honey babe mine, and see if the crawdads are biting." Or I might have said: "Let's really have some fun! You put on your old gray bonnet, the one with the blue ribbon on it, while I hitch old Dobbin to the buggy, and we'll take a buggy ride, and ride all over the fields of clover"! Now, don't you know that would have been lotsa fun!

But I wasn't a Southern gentleman, with a felt hat to tip. I was still just a boy, and boys didn't tip our caps to girls (I don't know why not. It looks like our paws would have taught us to follow in their footsteps; but they didn't).

And, by the time I got grown, and became a man, men had quit wearing hats. I never did learn what it would be like to tip my hat to a strange woman (I have a feeling that I have missed out on something). I have seen a lot of beautiful, gorgeous, dainty women that I would have loved to tip my hat to, if only I had a hat to tip. But I have saluted one or two, good lookers, and winked at a few, but they didn't nod back. Times have changed.

Oh! About Dick's hat band being too tight: It was paw's. Paw's name was Richard, and he was a real Southern gentleman. He wore his hat down to his eyebrows, but he still managed to tip it to all the women folks.

# CLICHÉ NO. 53

## WHAT'S IN THE WELL COMES UP IN THE BUCKET

People, in the old days, didn't have refrigerators, air conditioners, vacuum cleaners, and microwaves. They didn't have a lot of things that we take for granted today. They didn't even have running water, and those that were way out in the country didn't have electricity. Ask me. I know. I had to study my school lessons by the light of a kerosene lamp.

In those days, it was difficult to keep things from turning sour and spoiling.

Some people, who lived in town, were fortunate enough to have an ice box, and they made out pretty good, provided they didn't live too far from the icehouse. Those who lived in the little town of Iva, S.C. were very, very fortunate, because there was an iceman that came around, once a week delivering ice.

The iceman's name was "Rag" Robinson. I don't know how he got the name, "Rag". His britches were no more ragged than mine or anyone else's. In those days, a lot of people had patches on their britches, especially little boys. We shot marbles and would wear holes in our overalls, at the knees. Our mamas would patch our britches with cloths that were usually a different color (Well, it was hard to match faded out, blue denim overalls)!

Anyway, ole "Rag" would come around on Saturdays delivering ice. Saturday was the best day to deliver ice for every household would be serving iced tea on Sunday. At our house, we didn't have iced tea, except on Sundays. We drank buttermilk on other days.

I can see ole "Rag", now, on his ice-wagon. It was pulled by one of those big bobbed-tail, big footed, horses. "Rag" sat on a seat that reached clear across the wagon. The seat had a spring that was shaped like a bow. There was a saucer shaped, cast iron bell attached to the side of the wagon, near the driver's seat, and "Rag" would clang this bell and shout: "Ice-man! Ice-man!" You could here him coming, from a long ways off.

Our mamas would send us boys to meet him to buy ice. Usually, we bought a nickel's worth, or a dime's worth, and sometimes, a quarter's worth.

"Rag" would take an ice-pick and chip off, from a big block of ice that he carried on the wagon, the amount of ice you were buying, and then he would tie a burlap cord around the block of ice so that you could tote it back home.

A nickel's worth of ice was about six inches by six inches by twelve inches. A dime's worth was twice that amount. And a quarter's worth was a huge chunk that required two boys to carry. My mama seldom ever bought a quarter's worth. She didn't have the quarter. Her purchases were usually a nickel or dime; but that was enough ice for our tea.

Some country folks didn't have an ice box. They were like the Yankees and didn't know what iced tea was. These country folks, who lived way out in the sticks, used springs of water, and wells, to keep things cool.

I remember seeing such a spring, at the base of a big oak tree that had all kinds of things in it that a farm wife was trying to keep cool. Things like: A jar of buttermilk, a basket of eggs, watermelons, cantaloupes, and tomatoes, etc. There was a well worn path from the weather beaten, dilapidated, unpainted farm house to the spring.

After we moved to the country, away from the mill village, to a farm that was too far for the ice man to travel, we used our well to keep things cool. Many farmers used their wells for this purpose.

One time, "maw" sent me to the well to get a bucket of water and I got a surprise! The bucket was already down in the well and when I pulled it up, I found a half gallon jug of white lightning. "Paw" was using the well to keep his spirits cool. I took the jug of whiskey out of the bucket and let the bucket down in the well and got some water. Then, I put the whiskey back in the bucket and let it back down in the well. "Paw" never knew that I saw the whiskey. Another time, when I pulled the bucket up from the well, there was a black snake wrapped around the bucket handle. I let go of the windless and the bucket fell to the bottom of the well and made a big splash. When I pulled the buck up again, the snake was gone!

I tell you there's no telling what you might find in a country well. You have to wait until you draw the bucket up. What's in the well will come up in the bucket!

# CLICHÉ NO. 54

## LIKE A TREE PLANTED BY THE WATER

When I hear this cliché, I think back to my boyhood days, to the times "paw" would take us boys down to the muddy, rushing, mighty Savannah River. That river was always muddy and it was always rushing, and swift.

After "paw" had parked the Ford Touring car (the car without a top), we would walk down a shady, winding, oft trodden path down to the river. I guess it was about a half mile from where we parked to the river.

The path led by a big, cool, clear spring of water. We would always, never failing, stop and get a drink of that cool, clear water from that spring.

The spring had been there for eons of time. I don't know for how long, but I do know that it had to have been there for at least a hundred years. The white oak tree, that was located at the edge of the spring, was at least that old. It had a diameter of about four feet and it was a sprawling tree.

175

I think, also, that the big cool, clear spring of water was used by the American Indians, long before white men came here to disrupt and change, forever, their way of life. The reason that I think, and "paw" thought, and old Olin Taylor thought, and other ole timers thought that the spring was used by the Indians was because of the evidence that they left behind: One thing was a big boulder of a rock, nearby the spring. This boulder was about three feet high, with a dome shape above the ground, and had a hole in the top of the rock of about six inches in diameter and three inches deep. The old timers explained to me that the Indians utilized the hole in the big boulder to grind corn, or maize. They put the kernels in the hole and then they would pound the kernels, smash them, and grind them with a small rock, about the size of your double fist. I found a rock, near the spring, that I believe was used for this purpose.

There was, also, other evidence that Indians had used the spring: There was an old Indian graveyard, nearby, that had stones as grave markers. And we boys would always find (and we looked every time that we came) Indian arrowheads, and other relics.

That place, under the shade of that old oak tree, was a good campground for the Indians. I think that it must have been the Indians that planted that tree by the cool, clear, spring of water!

That old oak was not the only tree by the water, though. There were other trees, down on the banks of the Savannah, that were almost as large, and as old. There were huge alders, sweet- gums, pines, willows, water oaks, and all kinds.

Some of these huge trees leaned out over the river, and we boys had fun climbing them, as all boys will do, and going out on the limbs, and jumping in, and diving in (naked). Boys today don't know how to have fun like we country boys used to have. We played in the river, while "paw" went up the river to look his fish baskets.

Those trees had a whale of a big root system. The mesh of roots, on many of the trees near the banks, had been exposed by the waves of water sloshing over them for eons of time.

And another thing: Those trees, by the water, were not the only things that had big root systems. When I was a country farm boy, hoeing the grasses out of cotton, I noticed (I couldn't help but notice) that Johnson grass, and Bermuda grass and cuckel burrs had big root systems, too. (That must have been the way the cliché about "grass roots" got started. Some farm boy, having a heck of a time chopping cotton, started it). I tell you that it is no fun to hoe cotton, where there is a lot of Johnson grass, Bermuda grass, cuckle burrs, and honey suckles. These things are like trees planted by the water. They have big root systems. They are like a Southern boy, who was born and raised in the South. He has gotten his roots down. His roots are the "Grass Roots: of the South. You may take him out of the South (and some Yankee girls do), but you cannot, ever, take the South out of him!

But, do you know what? I was just thinking about how sad it is that there are just numerous people all over the world that don't have their roots down, anywhere. They are like the tumbleweed. They will tumble and roll and go where the wind blows. They get married and divorced, and marry again. They have no real foundation like good ole Southern boys have.

Some fight, and rage, and blow themselves up, and cause calamities and misery for the whole world simply because they have no real "grass roots"! They are easily provoked, and led astray by sadists, extremists, and ego maniacs, who are nothing but very shallow people.

I wish the whole world would be filled with people who have solid foundations, like a tree planted by the water, and not be moved come hell or high water!

# CLICHÉ NO. 55

## BURN YOUR BRIDGES BEHIND YOU

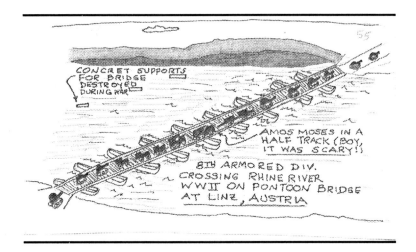

During World War II, when we were chasing the Nazi across France and Germany (they were retreating as fast a their German made vehicles could carry them), they destroyed all the bridges, after they had crossed over them; thus hoping that would slow the allied armies down, long enough, to give the Germans time to regroup and stand and fight again, but they underestimated the ingenuity of our combat engineers and navy sea bees.

When we arrived at a river that had no bridge, our combat engineers, and/or navy sea bees, would (like stirred up fire ants) get in the water with their motorboats, barges, and boom cranes, and in no time at all, have a temporary pontoon bridge floating in the water. I'm talking about a bridge strong enough, tough enough, and sturdy enough to handle heavy military loads, such as: trucks loaded with G.I.s, Sherman tanks, artillery with ten foot long barrels, mess trucks loaded with chow and cooking vessels, jeeps, halftracks, and big guns.

When we got to a river that had no bridge, we didn't have to tarry long, until we could cross over on a pontoon bridge, and pick up the pursuit, and be hot on the tail of those Germans again.

I remember (like yesterday) crossing such a bridge over the wide, sprawling, rushing, mighty Rhine River. It was scary for this ole Southern country boy. The biggest river that I had ever seen or crossed, 'til then, was the Savannah that divided South Carolina from Georgia, at Elberton and Iva. The Savannah was no wider than a football field. The Rhine was about ten or fifteen times the width of the Savannah. It was so wide that I could barely see across it!

And talking about swift: This big river was frightening swift, with all kinds of debris, from the war, floating in the river.

I had never crossed over a river on a pontoon bridge before. The only two bridges that I had ever crossed, the Sander's Ferry Bridge across the Savannah and a bridge across Wilson's creek, had frameworks of steel across the water and had wood floors, with some of the planks loose that would jump up and down and make a racket when a vehicle rolled over them.

The pontoon bridge, over the Rhine, was scary for this ole country boy. I held on tight to the door handles of the halftrack and gawked and looked in awe and wonder, and sweat some, too, as we crossed the river.

The bridge swayed, back and forth, up and down, and rattled and creaked and groaned. The bridge was so low that I could have reached and touched the water. Water would slosh over the sides and lap up onto the vehicles. I thought: Man, we are going to sink. What if the bridge comes apart, we will all get drowned out here in this big German river. But the bridge held together. The engineers did a good job of putting it together. We crossed over to dry land, picked up the scent of the German army, and started chasing them, again, at break neck speed.

Retreating armies burn their bridges behind themselves. They don't expect to have to come back that way, again. They burn bridges in hopes of getting some breathing room from their attacking enemies. They burn bridges to keep their enemies from putting their fighting machines out of business. They hope to live and fight again, somewhere and somehow.

I was just thinking: The roadway of life has many bridges that we must cross. And once we cross those bridges, we should burn them, and never come back over them again.

When we were little, our mamas went out and bought for us pencil boxes, crayons, pencils and paper, and we had to leave our mamas and start to school. That's a bridge in life. That bridge was kind of like that pontoon bridge that I had to cross. It was scary. But we crossed that bridge. We couldn't quit and go back home, but we had to keep on going to get an education.

When my brother started to school, the first day, he jumped out a window and went back home. He crossed back over that bridge; but my mama made him to go back to school. In effect, she burned that bridge; he couldn't go back over it again. He had to stay in school, whether he liked it or not.

There should come a time in everyone's life when we finish school, when we finish our education, and then get out and go to work (though some folks never do. They go to school all the days of their lives. They are afraid to cross over that bridge that leads to work). Some folks are satisfied with others doing all the work. They never contribute to the needs of others. They do not pull their share of the load in society.

There are some that are mamas' boys all the days of their lives. They cannot accept the responsibility of leaving home, getting married (a bridge in life) and starting a family (another bridge) and raising kids and being a daddy or mama, and changing their diapers, wiping their noses, tying their shoes, taking them to church, seeing to it that they do their homework, and get an education.

That's three bridges in the roadway of life (there are others): The bridge of leaving mama and going to school, the bridge of finishing our education and going to work, the bridge of getting married and raising a family. These bridges should be burned after we cross them, because we don't want to come that way again.

Agree or disagree? Amen or oh me?

# CLICHÉ NO. 56

## SLIM PICKINGS

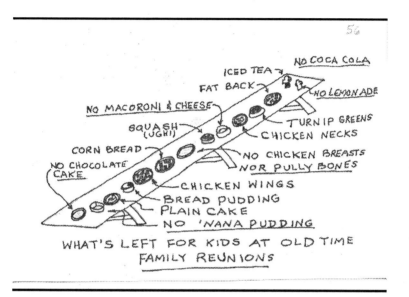

NO COCA COLA
ICED TEA
FAT BACK
NO LEMONADE
NO MACORONI & CHEESE
SQUASH (UGH!)
TURNIP GREENS
CHICKEN NECKS
CORN BREAD
NO CHICKEN BREASTS
NO CHOCOLATE CAKE
NOR PULLY BONES
CHICKEN WINGS
BREAD PUDDING
PLAIN CAKE
NO 'NANA PUDDING

WHAT'S LEFT FOR KIDS AT OLD TIME
FAMILY REUNIONS

If you happen to be a young person reading this, I want to tell you again, again, and again, until you get the message (It doesn't seem that you are getting the message that we old folks keep telling you). That message is: You don't know how lucky you are!!

Why, when I was a boy, I had to pick cotton, plow a mule, walk five miles to catch a bus to go to school.............Ah, what's the use, I won't go into that all over again. I know that you're not listening, anyway!

But, what I do want to talk to you about, this time, if you will listen and pay attention, and if I haven't already told you umpteen times before, is about the family reunions back when children should be seen but not heard.

We would gather down at my grandpa's house. My grandma had died when I was a baby, so I don't know how the family reunions were before then.

There were lots of aunts and uncles, in-laws, and cousins (must have been at least a hundred fifty people), and all of them brought big appetites with them. That's the way most country folks stayed back then. They stayed hungry.

And I hate to tell you this (Lord, I'm ashamed to admit it), but most of my kinfolks (all except my mama) were, you know, "hoggish". And I told a cousin so, one time when he was visiting us. I was just a little fellow and said anything that came on my mind. I told him: "Boy, you sure do eat hoggish"! I know that wasn't polite to talk that way to a visitor, but I felt like someone should tell him about his poor manners.

All these country women, my mama's side of the family, brought big baskets of food, and put the dishes on a long table, out in the yard. When it was time to eat, the grown folks got to eat first. We children had to go a play and wait for the grown ups to finish eating. They would call us when it was time for us to eat.

That's the part, right here, that I want to talk to you young folks about, again. I repeat: You don't know how lucky you are!

When my grown-up kin folks started eating, they were worse than "finger licking" Italians, eating spaghetti. They were worse than a bunch of wild hyenas stealing meat from the buzzards. I hate to say it, but they acted like cavemen from the dark ages when everyone would eat grub worms, lizards, insects, you name it, they would eat it. They had no manners.

When they finally called us children and told us that we could fix our plates, there was not much left. There were no fried chicken legs. It looks to me like they would have saved all the chicken legs for the children, but they didn't. And, further more, as for as fried chicken was concerned, the only pieces that were left were chicken necks, backs, and wings.

That's what I call: "Slim Pickings"!

Young folks, you don't know how lucky you are with your souped up Mustangs. You can go prowling around malls on Saturday nights, with money in your pockets, a girl friend on each arm, and with your cell phone to your ear and mouth and talking to another one.

Back in my boyhood days, young folks thought it was something to get to go to town with "maw" and "paw" on Saturdays and get a hotdog and a Pepsi Cola. Young folks, back in my days, weren't allowed to talk, and have money, and have fun. The pickings were slim, back then.

I guess that's one reason why children seem to be spoiled and rotten today: Their parents don't want to see their children have to suffer the hardships that they, the parents, went through when they were young.

I know that's so with me. I cannot, for the life of me, understand why parents (my "paw" was guilty) treated their children mean. They would say: "Shut up! Don't you know that you're not supposed to talk when grown ups are talking? Get up! Get out of that bed! The sun is an hour high! If you don't do what I say, I will get a stick to you!" And they would, too. I stayed afraid of my "paw" and that ought not to be!

But, I hand it to my "maw". She had a difficult life. She had her hands full with all her younguns and a cantankerous husband. But she had enough love, in her heart, for everyone.

At our house, when we had fried chicken on Sundays, "paw" would get the breast, and we children had our pick of the rest, and "maw" would eat the back or the neck or the wing. She was the one to get the slim pickings.

Young folks listen. I want to tell you one more time: "You don't know how lucky you are." But I'm glad for you. I'm glad your pickings are much better than mine were.

# CLICHÉ NO. 57

## HAVING AXES TO GRIND

Every farmer, in the old days, down South, had a blacksmith's shop. And there was a blacksmith's shop down town, in Iva, near where the old jailhouse stands today. This shop was a busy place, especially on Saturdays, when farmers would come to town to get their mules shod. That's one thing that farmers could not do was to put shoes on their mules. It took an expert blacksmith to do that, and Iva had such a smith that knew how to put new mules' shoes on mules. (I've watched him do it, many times).

It was fun watching him. He would bend over, and straddle the mule's leg, and lift the mule's hoof between his knees, and then use a draw knife, which was a knife with two handles with a sharp blade between the handles, and cut the bottom of the hoof so that it was flat and even and wide enough to install a steel shoe on the mule's hoof.

He would measure the hoof, put the mule's hoof back down, and then go to his many mule shoes hanging on a wall in his shop, and select the shoe that came closest to meeting the dimensions of the mule's hoof.

He would never find a shoe that fit the hoof exactly. So, he would fire up the forge, using charcoal or sometimes plain coal. He would turn the handle on the blower, that blew air under the fire, and the coals would glow and become white hot. When the coals were really glowing, he would stick the horseshoe (oops, the mule shoe) in the fire, under the coals, using smith's tongs.

After the mule shoe became red hot, he would pull it out of the fire, with tongs, take it to an anvil and use a sharp chisel to trim the ends off the shoe. Then, he would hold the shoe with the tongs, turn it, and bend it, and flatten the shoe, with a big hammer, to fit the mule's hoof. We boys would pick up the nuggets, that the smith had trimmed off of the mules' shoes, and use the nuggets as ammo in our sling shots when shooting at squirrels, rats, birds, tin cans and other targets.

After the smith had shaped the shoe just right, he would dip it in a big tub of water to cool it, then he would go back to the mule, bend over with his back to the mule's leg, lift the hoof and put it between his knees, and install the mule shoe using sharp pointed nails driven at an angle to the outside of the hoof. He would clip off the excess nails that protruded outside the hoof.

After he had installed shoes on all four hooves, he would have the mule walk around to see how the mule liked his new shoes. Usually, the mules would walk kind of stiff legged, until they got used to the new shoes. (Like country boys, who had been going barefooted all summer, had to put on shoes, when the weather got cold).

Like I said: Farmers brought their mules to town to have shoes put on them, but the farmers could usually handle other blacksmith's jobs in their own shops. For example: They could sharpen plows, put new handles in hoes, shovels, and pitch forks. They could sharpen hoes (needed to have sharp hoes for chopping cotton), and sharpen axes for all the wood chopping going on around the farms.

The black smith shop, with the fire, forge, and anvil, was used for sharpening plows. A good blacksmith had a rhythm, when sharpening plows. I can hear "paw" now, down in his blacksmith shop, sharpening a plow. He would heat the plow red hot, bring it to the anvil with tongs, and place the edge of the plow on the anvil. He would then hit the cutting edge of the plow a lick with the hammer, and then hit the anvil two licks. The sound of his hammer would sound something like this: Pow! Ping, Ping! Pow! Ping, Ping! He would turn the plow this way, and that way.

And repeat the action (one lick to the plow and two licks to the anvil) until he had the plow sharp. The best smiths had the best rhythm in hitting the plow and the anvil.

All farms had grindstones for sharpening hoes, shovels, and axes. "Paw" used his grindstone a lots for sharpening his ax. Wood was the chief fuel, back in those days, and we burned a lot of it.

"Paw" kept his ax sharp at all times. He didn't allow it to get dull. When he wasn't using it, he kept it sunk into a stump near the woodpile, so that he would have it handy for the next time he had to cut a load of wood.

All farms had woodpiles. All farms had blacksmith shops. All farms had grindstones. All farms had axes to grind.

People today don't have axes to grind nearly as much as they used to have, because people of today don't have woodpiles.

Maybe the day is coming when no one will have an axe to grind. Hey! Wouldn't that be good??

# CLICHÉ NO. 58

## DON'T STRADDLE THE FENCE

Fences are used to hold animals. It is not intended that fences be used for holding people.

That's what is so great about America. Over here, we don't fence people in. America is a land of opportunity. Over here, people are not restricted, except in a few cases where governmental bureaucrats think they know more than we do about what we want and need.

But, in the early days, America had very few fences. People were free to roam, and go, and settle where ever they chose. Back then, America was frontier land (most of it).

The first settlements were in the northeast. Then, after cities sprang up, some settlers were not happy with city life. They were too hemmed in, especially those who were country folks: The farmers, hunters, and those who liked the wide-open spaces.

The frontiers quickly moved to the South (naturally), and to the West in rushes. Some homesteaders were given forty acres and a mule (that was a pretty good deal for some of my descendents), and some went westward to strike it rich, when gold was discovered in California, and they did just that, and they stayed there until this day and they are filthy rich.

The first pioneers suffered many hardships. Most of them were courageous people who loved freedom and opportunity, but there were some that were rotten eggs. These are the ones who wanted to get rich quick, whether it was by hook or crook. It didn't make any difference. They were not satisfied with working and earning their own way. They schemed and pilfered from those who did work (same way that some folks do today).

There were cattle rustlers, looters, robbers, arsonists, and a lot of lawlessness that caused many hardships and wastes for the pioneers.

The cowboy movies of the wild and untamed west were not far wrong in depicting the way of life for the early American pioneers.

As the frontiers moved southward and westward, and as small communities and towns began to spring up along the way, railways had to be extended across America.

Herds of cattle, buffalo, horses, and other animals were allowed to roam free. There were no fences, just wide open spaces.

In the beginning, railway companies installed cow-catchers (an inverted "V" shaped metal frame) on the front of the steam engines that would push the cattle and buffalo off the tracks, without killing the animals, so as to keep the trains from jumping the tracks.

The cow-catchers seemed to work for a while, but more and more animals came to graze along the railway tracks, until it got to where there were so many animals on the tracks that trains had to slow down to a creeping crawl. More drastic measures had to be taken. That's when fences came into being in America.

The railway companies, Pacific and others, began to install fences, barbwire fences of all things, along the railway tracks. These fences infuriated the settlers. Many got their guns, six shooters and muzzle-loaders, and dared the train companies to install fences across their lands. Well, the train companies hired lawyers to go to Washington to talk to the politicians and try to put a stop to the settlers shooting at their fence installers!

I guess politicians will always be politicians and there was not much difference back then. Most of the politicians were lawyers from the cities and had never heard of a barbed wire fence. They didn't know what a barbed wire fence was, but they acted like they knew all about it. Have you ever seen a politician that didn't know all about anything and everything?

Well, the politicians, at first had to straddle the barbed wire fence. They had to test the waters (like we boys used to test the waters with our big toe before jumping in naked to go skinny dipping). The politicians wanted to see which way the wind was blowing back home before they voted to allow the train companies to install the barbed wire fences.

In the end, the train companies had more money than the poor settlers, so the politicians quit straddling the barbed wire fences, and voted to send federal marshals out to protect the railway workers. The fences got installed.

If those politicians were still alive, I'm sure they would tell you that straddling a barbed wire fence is no fun and if there is anyway around the fence, take it. But, in this case, I'm glad the politicians made a decision. Sometimes, they will go on forever straddling fences and you never know where they stand.

I'm also glad that America had those frontiersmen who put up a fight. They were people of courage, of individualism, optimistic, love of freedom, sure-footed, country folks. They were the backbone of America.

I'm glad to be and American. Aren't you?

# CLICHÉ NO. 59

## THE RUN OF THE MILL

Southern farm boys, back when I was one, were raised on beans and cornbread. That was our main vittles. Sometimes, we would get black-eyed peas or purple hull crowder peas instead of the beans (pintos, usually); but we always, never failing, got cornbread.

Southern mamas, most of the time, put cracklings in the cornbread. That's what made the cornbread taste so good. If you have never eaten cornbread, with the cornmeal ground by rocks and a water wheel, and with cracklings, you don't know what you have been missing.

Our cornbread, including the cracklings, was home grown. (That's another thing that made the cornbread taste so good). If you get out and work your "tail" off from sun-up 'til sun-down, with a little time off at noon for some beans and cornbread, you are hungry as a horse, and anything will taste good (even fatback and black molasses. I ate a lot of that, too).

It's a fact of life. If you work and earn something (anything) with your own hands, you will get a lot more enjoyment out of it than you would if somebody else gave you something for free.

We worked and earned our cornbread. We worked and earned our beans, and peas. We worked (I did the sloping of our hogs) and earned the cracklings that made the cornbread so good. We plowed the fields, fertilized the ground, with a guano, mule drawn fertilizer distributor, planted the kernels of corn, with a mule drawn corn planter, plowed the corn, with a mule drawn plow that had sweeps and a fender to keep from covering up the corn, when it first peeped through the ground, pulled the corn, with our hands, and put the corn in a burlap sack that had a shoulder strap, and when the sack got full of corn, we took it and emptied it in a wagon pulled by two mules, and hauled the corn to the corn cribs.

Then, on rainy days, when we couldn't work outside, we went to the corncribs and shucked corn. Oh happy day! That was fun time with my brothers. With the rain beating down on the tin roof, we could just sit, for a change, and crack jokes (my brother "Dub" was full of them. I could probably tell you some that I learned from "Dub", but they would be too raunchy). We would shuck corn and throw the ears of corn in one pile and the shucks in another. We fed the shucks to our cow. She liked them.

It was fun, too, taking the corn to Burris's mill to grind into cow feed, chicken feed, and corn meal. The mill had a great big water wheel with two big, round granite rocks for grinding the corn. For the cow feed, we ground the corn, cobs and all. That's what you call the run of the mill. Everything was in the cow feed, even sweepings from the floor. For the chicken feed, we first shelled the corn. The mill had a corn sheller. The miller set the huge grinding stones differently to grind chicken feed, and the corn was cracked into little pieces, chicken feed sizes, by the granite rocks.

For corn meal, the miller brought the grinding rocks closer together, with a lever, sifted the grindings, and the result was corn meal, fit to be made into cornpone.

Mister Burris would take a fourth of what ever he was grinding for his fee. The milled product, whether it be cow feed

191

(run of the mill), chicken feed, or corn meal, ended up in a cylindrical container with markings showing the volume. Mister Burris would scoop out a fourth (seemed kinda high for his little bit of work compared to ours, but that was the way it was. He did have a lot of money invested in that big water wheel, the dam, chute, and machinery).

The cow feed was the least refined. It was the run of the mill. The corn meal was the most refined. Kinda like, I think, graduates of Old Iva High. Some of them (most of them) were the run of the mill. Please don't get me wrong. I think they did well, but most of them didn't go further with their education, and study, and didn't really exert themselves, and work their "tails" off for a season, so that they could get the best jobs and climb the ladder to success. Most chose to be the run of the mill type. Some did a little better, but they were still chicken feed.

Others, only a few, went to college and studied and burned the midnight oil and crammed their heads full of knowledge and became (I know I'm biased) the cream of the crop!

# CLICHÉ NO. 60

## WEATHERING THE STORMS

I'm sure glad that I don't live in "tornado alley": Kansas, Oklahoma, and Nebraska. And I know that "paw" was glad that he didn't have to live there. He was scared to death of the least little thunderstorm.

But of course, he had a pretty good reason to be scared of storms. If you could have seen the rickety old house that we lived in, you would understand.

It wouldn't have taken much of a wind to blow that old house to kingdom's come. We could lie in bed, at night, and count the stars. And we could feed the chickens that were under the house through cracks in the floor.

Maybe I'm exaggerating a little, but most country shacks, that were way out in the sticks like ours, were rickety. That's the reason that most country families had a storm cellar that they could flee to, when storms came up.

Our storm cellar was a simple one. It was a ten feet by ten feet hole in the ground with dirt pilled on top of a tin roof. Our cellar had a door which leaned at about a thirty degree angle, and had steps, carved out in the dirt. It contained wood benches around the wall where we could sit until the storms passed over. The shelter had no windows. It was dark in there. It was spooky in there. You can imagine how scary it was for children, like me, to have to sit in that spooky place and listen to the winds howling and rattling things outside. We used that shelter many times, when I was a youngster, for my "paw", who I thought wasn't scared of anything, not even a snake, got scared stiff when thunder clouds began to roll. We didn't have TV's back then to watch. We didn't even have a radio. We didn't even have electricity. So we didn't get any news about tornados, severe thunderstorms, or windstorms in our area. "Paw" was our weatherman.

I don't know why "paw" was so scared of thunder. "Maw" wasn't. Sometimes, she wouldn't even go with us when "paw" came running and took us little ole boys to the storm cellar. She would say: "Ah, "paw", ain't no need. That storm will pass over." And sure 'nough it would, always, every time. Not once, did we come out of that cellar to find the house or barn blown away.

I remember, while sitting in that cellar, with slithers of light through the cracks in the door, seeing "paw" fear stricken. He was scared to death. He was as nervous as an old setting hen, and I don't know why. Iva, up until that time, had never had a tornado in the town's history. So, I don't believe "paw" was afraid that the house would get blown away. That old house had weathered many storms.

It is very, very puzzling for me to understand my "paw". Hey! Wait a minute! I think I've got it! I think I know why "paw" was afraid of thunderstorms: "Paw" felt guilty!" He didn't have the faith that "maw" had. You know, the faith that helps people to weather all sorts of storms, come what may, in their lives.

"Paw" was afraid that the Lord might zap him with a lightning bolt. He had been a rough character, drinking all that moonshine and stuff.

That's the reason that he would run and hide when storm clouds rolled. He had not confessed his sins, and he wasn't ready to be zapped!

# CLICHÉ NO. 61

## OVER THE HILL

Over the hill and through the woods to grand mama's house we go. The horse knows the way to carry the sleigh....etc. That's a Yankee tune. I know it's Yankee, because we have never used sleighs down South. We used mules and wagons, back in those days. But, like the horse, our mules did know the way, not to grand mama's house, but back to their home, back to their stables in the barn, back home to some good vittles of oats and corn on the cob.

After we had gotten up early, fed the mules, and fed ourselves with grits and eggs and some good ole country ham, and after we had gone back to the barn and put bridles on the mules, and led them out of their stables, and put the gear on them (collars, traces, back bands and all), and after we had backed the mules (two of'em) up to the wagon and hooked the traces to the single trees (double trees for two mules), and after we had said: "Get up" to the mules, and after they had quit balking (they were still sleepy) and started pulling together and pulled the wagon out of the lean-to-shed and up to the cotton house door, and after we had climbed out of the wagon (I know this is a long sentence, but I don't want to leave anything out. I want you to get the whole picture) and went into the cotton house, which was filled to the ceiling with cotton that we had hand picked ourselves, and after we (two of us boys) had gotten our baskets and filled them with cotton and carried the baskets, on our shoulders, to the wagon and dumped the cotton into the wagon, where one of us had stayed to spread the cotton out evenly, with our feet, and packed it down good, and after we had loaded the wagon to the top of the side bodies, we, then, all of us, climbed aboard and said to the mules, again: "Get up", and after the mules stopped balking again(they had gone back to sleep while we were loading the cotton), and started straining (the load of cotton was heavy) and started pulling together, and after we had taken that load of cotton all the way from our cotton house to the gin house in Iva, about six miles, and after we said: "whoa" to the mules, when the load of cotton was under the suction chute at the gin house, and after we had taken that big cylindrical suction chute tube and sucked all the cotton out of the wagon, and after the cotton was ginned into a 500 pound bale, and after we had sold that bale of cotton to Mister Press Gaily for 25 cents per pound, it was time to go back home and put our mules back in the barn (Whew! I've done run out of steam).

We said: "get up" to the mules again, and they didn't balk this time. They knew where we were going, and they knew the way, and we didn't even have to guide them. They were going home, and we could not hold them back! It didn't take much to make our mules homesick (a day at the gin, in Iva, away from their home in the barn, was enough).

But of course, I can sympathize with the mules. They were country. They had lived in the country all of their lives. Country and city does not mix. When you take country mules (or country boys for that matter) out of the country, and put them in a city (even a little city, like Iva), they can't wait to get back to their home in the sticks. That's the way our mules were and that's the way this ole country boy is.

"Over the hill and through the woods" that's country. Even though it's a Yankee tune, believe it or not, there are some

Yankees that are country (I've seen some): Midianites, with their buggies, and big barns, and women in long dresses, and men with Abraham Lincoln style beards (how country can you get?), way up there in the Yankee country of Pennsylvania. These people (I hate to say it. Lord, I hate to say it) may be more country than me and other Southerners. These people still drive horses and buggies. I drive a convertible (it makes me feel young). They don't have electricity. They still use kerosene lamps (if my TV goes on the blink for five minutes, I'm upset with the TV station, the satellite people, my wife, her cat, my neighbors, everything). They still cook on stoves that burn wood. My wife cooks on an electric stove, in a microwave, in a crock- pot, and we eat out half of the time.

You know, after thinking about it, I'm not nearly as country as I thought I was. I enjoy all the conveniences of modern day life. But, I do still enjoy taking a ride, on Sundays, not in a mule and wagon or in a horse drawn sleigh, but in my convertible over the hill and through the woods. And I listen to country music (life is but a dream) on my car radio.

# CLICHÉ NO. 62

## KICKING THE HABIT

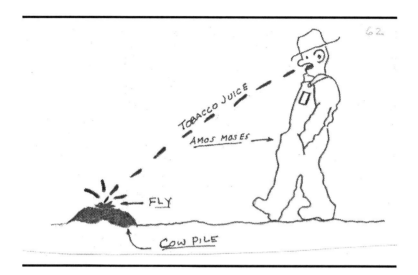

A habit is something that a girl wears, when she is riding side-saddle on a horse so that her underwear doesn't show. Don't try to kick that habit. You might get your face slapped and you would deserve it. That's not the type of habit that I'm talking about that you should kick.

The type of habit that I'm proposing you to kick is the other kind, like the chewing tobacco habit. Now, that's a habit that everyone should kick, even baseball players (unless, the umpires are blind, and doesn't know the difference between balls and strikes, then it's alright for baseball players to chew tobacco, and to spit tobacco juice on the umpires' shoes, too. That's alright. That's part of the game. That takes some of the dullness, not all of it, but some, out of baseball games).

But, little boys should definitely not chew tobacco, even if their daddies chew, and their uncles chew, and (oh me) even if their mamas chew.

If you have the habit of chewing tobacco, kick it! Kick it out the door! Kick it down the street! Kick it so far that it will never come back to pester you again! Kick it while you are young. Kick it while you are alive! Kick it while you still have your teeth, before you would have to give a snaggletooth grin.

Kick the habit of chewing tobacco while you are still able to find a pretty little, dainty, Southern lass, to hug, and to kiss. Southern lasses are special. They deserve to be kissed by real Southern gentlemen, who have brushed their teeth, and used dental floss, and mouth spray before going out on a date. Southern lasses don't want to be kissed by someone who chews tobacco, and drools the juice from the corners of his mouth (ugh!), and maybe get some of it on her Sunday dress.

If you are weak and cannot bring yourself to kick the habit, then you probably will have to find yourself a girl that chews, too. And both of you will wind up with no teeth! (Ugh, again). What kind of kiss would that be, huh? "Smack"! "Oh"! I think I just swallowed my teeth!! Just to be on the safe side, both of you might have to take your teeth out, especially if you are passionately in love (ha! ha!).

I'm glad to report that most little boys have kicked the chewing tobacco habit. I don't see nearly as many boys that chew today like they did in my boyhood days living on the mill hill. I think I know the reason. It's because their daddies, and uncles, and mamas don't chew.

But, I have a confession to make: When I was a little ole barefooted country boy, knee high to a grasshopper, I chewed. My "paw" chewed, and I thought that was a manly thing to do (little boys try to be like their daddies).

My "paw" chewed "Full Bloom" chewing tobacco. He bought plugs of it. A plug was about 3 inches wide by about 8 inches long by about ½ inch thick. He kept his chewing tobacco in the kitchen safe drawer (that's an old type china cabinet). When "paw" ran out of tobacco, he would go to the safe and cut a half plug off and stick it in the bib of his overalls.

Sometimes, I would go to that safe drawer and cut myself off a sliver of "paw's" tobacco and put it in my jaw (like "paw") and spit tobacco juice (like "paw"). And I got to be pretty good at spitting. I could hit a fly, sometimes, on a cow pile, as far away as 10 feet (that's a pretty good shot).

Well, I'm ashamed to admit it, but I got the habit. I got addicted. I began to save my pennies and when I got enough (I think 10 cents), I would go to the Dixie Store and buy myself a small plug of "Bloodhound" chewing tobacco (other boys would buy ice cream, but I would buy chewing tobacco), and, sometimes, one of those boys who had bought ice cream with his money, would see me coming, and he would always, without failing, bum a chew from me (I didn't think it fair, but I would give the bum a chew, because it was more fun having someone to chew with and see who could spit the farthest, etc.).

I don't remember exactly when I quit chewing. I think it was probably after I had my first date, when I was about fifteen. A little girl (the one that asked me to marry her when I was sixteen) sent word to me by another boy (while I was laying my head in the lap of another girl, on my school bus, waiting for the bus driver to quit yapping and take us home) that she would like a date with me. (How about that? I must have been handsome, and I know, that I know, that she didn't know that I chewed tobacco, else she would not have asked me for a date).

So it was, about then, that I came to my senses and decided that to have a pretty little, nice, dainty, southern Belle to hug and to kiss was more important than chewing tobacco.

I kicked the habit! And I'm glad, for ever more that I did, for I don't have to give a snaggletooth grin and neither does my wife!

# CLICHÉ NO. 63

## LIT UP LIKE A CHRISTMAS TREE

This must be a fairly new cliché for I can remember (and I don't consider myself all that old) when Christmas trees did not have lights.

Christmas celebrations were a lot different back then, and I think a lot more fun. In those days, if you were going to have a Christmas tree (and a lot of folks didn't), you would have to go to the woods and cut a tree, a cedar. You couldn't go to Walmarts or to Targets and buy a plastic tree, and after Christmas, put the tree in a box and save it for next Christmas.

The reason you couldn't do this was because there were no Walmarts, and there were no Targets, and there were no plastic Christmas trees, period.

You had to get out of the house, and go cut your own tree, and haul it in a wagon, or on top of a car, if you were lucky enough to have a car, and bring the tree home, and nail it to a plank on the bottom, so that the tree would stand on its own, and select a spot by the window, so that the neighbors could see it in the day time, and dress it up with home ornaments.

It was fun for our family to pile into "paw's' "A" model (the car without a top) and go to the woods to find the perfect cedar to use for our Christmas tree.

All of us, even us boys, felt that we had a part in selecting the tree. We would point this one out (too big), and that one (too short), and that one (not enough limbs), and that one. "Oh well, I guess that one will do" mama would say (it was her decision all the time). "Let's cut it." And "paw" would get his hand- saw (chain saws had not been invented), and he would get down on his knees, and he would saw the tree off a few inches above the ground.

We would tie the tree, with a burlap cord (we used a lot of burlap cords, back then) to the side of the "A" model touring car (the one that had no top), and we would gleefully pile in and go home, laughing all the way!

Yes, we had to cut our own Christmas tree. And furthermore, we could not buy the ornaments, except for aluminum slivers for ice-cycles and maybe an angel and a star. We had to make our own ornaments. Well, my mama and my sisters did. "Paw" and us boys would just get in the way and mess things up, if we tried to help. And I'm telling you, the trinkets that they made were just beautiful, and that, my friends, was a lot of fun, too, watching them make those beautiful things with nothing but waxed paper, crayons, and maybe water colors, a pair of scissors, staples, and tape. They made: birds (doves, blue birds, geese, swans, ducks, and chickens), animals (sheep, horses, deer, pigs, and cows), fruit (apples, oranges, grapes, plum grannies, and pears), people (little Dutch girls, pilgrims, and Indians), Christ, and angels, and stars, and moon, and sun.

Then, they would hang those things on the tree, along with the store bought aluminum ice-cycles and maybe a star or an angel at the top of the tree. When they had finished decorating the tree, they would stand back, and "paw" and us boys would join them, and admire the Christmas tree, with all the decorations that their own hands had created. That was lots of fun!

We didn't have very many gifts, wrapped in Christmas paper, to go under the tree. Money was as scarce as hen's teeth, but the few gifts that we did receive, we knew were bought with hard earned money, and we knew the gifts were given with heart felt love. Love means much more than money, any day. Love was what made our Christmases so special. You could feel the spirit of love in the air at Christmas time!

It wasn't until later, after Bing Crosby sang: "I'm dreaming of a white Christmas, just like the ones I used to know. Where tree tops glistened, and children listened to hear sleigh bells in the snow." I know that's a Yankee tune, because we didn't have many white Christmases down south, and I don't remember ever hearing sleigh bells in the snow, but the part "just like the ones I used to know" was as much down South Southern as it was Yankee, Christmas began to change.

People began to make more money. Mamas and sisters quit making Christmas tree ornaments. "Paw", "maw" and the kids quit going out into the woods together to cut a Christmas tree. Everyone got too busy at doing their own thing. Stores began selling factory made in China Christmas ornaments, and plastic Christmas trees (made in China, too). Christmas even quit smelling like Christmas.

Then it happened! REA started running electric lines to homes out in the sticks. The whole country became electrified! Electric lights began popping up all over the South.

People even started hanging lights on Christmas trees. At first, the lights were about the size of your thumb, and then the lights became smaller and smaller, wee, wee small and blinking!

Now they hang Christmas lights everywhere: all over the eaves of houses, all over shrubbery, all over trees, everywhere.

I saw a place like that out in the boondocks, way out in the sticks, with lights everywhere, even down to the creek, and that's not all I saw (I couldn't believe my eyes), lo and behold, there was a lady walking around out there in the dark with Christmas tree lights wrapped around her body! Talking about fantasy, she was lit up like a Christmas tree!

I wish Christmas would be like it used to be, when the only thing lit up was "paw" after drinking his moonshine. He was a whole lot more fun and Christmas was, too.

# CLICHÉ NO. 64

## JUST A BIG BAG OF WIND

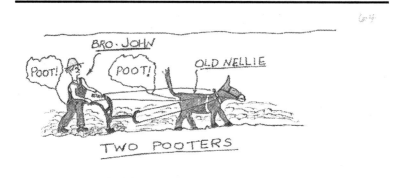

I know that this is a Southern cliché. We used to hear it a lots down South, so I know that we must have invented it.

There was a guy, my next-door neighbor, who was the biggest fool that you have ever seen. He was such a big fool that we neighborhood boys nicknamed him "Goofy" (I'm not going to tell you his real name, because it might embarrass his children).

This fellow was a grown man, when I was still a boy. But, he was always hanging around with us boys and cutting the fool.

I remember that one time he told us: "I can poot anytime that I want to." I said: "Okay, let me hear you poot." He said: "I don't want to right now." Ha! Ha! No, seriously, he could generate a poot at any time. (And you didn't even have to pull his finger). He showed us that he could do it, more than once (I would say, at least umpteen times).

He was really goofy. And what I call: "Just a big bag of wind!"

I knew another fellow that was a big bag of wind. He could poot, also. But he was not like Goofy.

This fellow would poot when he didn't want to. He was my next-door neighbor, when I lived down in Georgia. He and his wife came over to our house, one cold wintry night for a visit. I had a blazing fire going in the fireplace (all country boys like log fires). My wife and I and he and his wife were sitting in my den and chit chatting.

The fire had died down, somewhat, and he decided that it was time to throw another log on the fire. He went over beside the fireplace to get a log, and when he bent over to get the log, he let go a big one. He looked at us kind of sheepishly and grinned, and his wife said: "Huh! Ooh!" (He was another big bag of wind).

I'll tell you of another couple bags of wind, and I'll shut up.

I used to work with an engineer on a Naval training project at Dam Neck, Virginia. This fellow was called by his nickname "Poot King" (his last name was his real name). One of the pretty, nice, feminine, dainty secretaries in our office asked me how he got a nick- name like that. I said: "I guess it was because he was a big bag of wind when he was a boy ."

My mama wouldn't allow us boys to poot in the house. If we wanted to poot, we had to go out in the barn with the other pooters (the mules. They ate corn that made them poot. We ate beans), or to some place else where no one would hear us. It's not very nice to poot in public. But some people do just that.

There was a policeman that we had in Iva at one time. He was down at the ice-house where Mister Pringle Clinksgales sold ice to the public. The policeman's nick name was "Scrap Iron". He carried two great big Smith and Western pistols on his belt.

Well, a bunch of us boys used to hang out down there. The colored attendant, Wilkes Hall, didn't mind. He had fun with us, when he wasn't pulling those big blocks of ice out of the tanks that were in the floor. Scrap Iron was down there one night. He was an uncouth sort of a fellow. He strutted, or waddled like a duck, with his chest stuck out. He acted to me like he thought he was it, like he was the boss of Iva, or the king of the jungle. You've seen people like that. They have such a high opinion of themselves that they think they can do anything (even poot in public)!

Scrap Iron did and I heard it! How revolting! How repulsive!! How disgusting! How raunchy! Just who does he think he is? I would have liked to give him a big kick in the butt, but I was just a little ole cotton mill boy!

When I went home, I told my brother "Dub" about old Scrap Iron, down at the ice-house, pooting in his britches. "Dub" just laughed and said: "Do you think he should have pulled his britches down to poot?"

I'm just a country boy, and I know that I don't know all the rules and regulations of proper etiquette; but there is one thing that I feel I do know "you are not supposed to poot in public." Only fools and big bags of wind would do that!

The South used to be full of raunchy, uncouth people like "Goofy" and "Scrap Iron", but we don't have nearly as many such fools today. Hardly ever do you hear one poot in public. Maybe it's because we have quit eating so many beans. There are not nearly as many big bags of wind around today, and that's good!

# CLICHÉ NO. 65

## THAT'S JUST DUCKY

You know how ducks walk. They walk bowl legged and twist their hind end. I had a high school teacher that walked like that, and she did have a big hind end, but she was the nicest, and sweetest, and best teacher that I had. (Hey, that's not her that I have depicted, here. She looked better than that). She had never been married (lady teachers had to be single, back then). I guess that she had resolved to never get married, because she was in her thirties. I think that her main interest in life was to be the best teacher that she could possibly be, and in my opinion, she had accomplished just that.

And do you know something? It seemed that all of my teachers were like that (I'm not talking about walking like a duck. I'm talking about being the best teachers that they could possibly be). I still remember each one of them. They left an indelible mark on my life (but it was a good mark, a good memory). I can name each one of my teachers, from the first grade through the eleventh grade, but I won't (we only had eleven grades), and I can describe every one of them: Nice, pleasant, charming, loving. I would say that they all were: "just ducky" (ever last one).

But it was different when I went to college. I wouldn't say that my college professors were "just ducky". I would say they were more like "mister grumpy". The college professors (that's what they wanted to be called and not teachers) didn't take a hands-on personal interest in each student as did my public school teachers. The college professors would throw it at you, and they didn't care if you caught it or not. They left it up to you to grasp all that you could get.

My public school teachers were down to earth (Christian in most cases), who genuinely cared for each student. They felt that they were responsible for imparting, to their students, more than book knowledge, but social knowledge, spiritual knowledge, knowledge of morals, decency, and good citizenship as well (and the Lord knows that we poor little ole raunchy cotton mill boys needed all this type knowledge that we could soak up).

College professors, in most cases, were PhD's, eggheads, highbrows, bookworms, intellectuals, who did not enjoy the simple things in life, and they seemed to care less if the students learned anything or not.

Those with PhD degrees (and Lord, I know that they must have worked hard to earn that degree) didn't want their students, and anybody else, to forget that they had a PhD. They insisted that you address them as "doctor". They were "ed-u-ca-tors" and they didn't want you to forget it! Intellectualism was the most important thing in their lives. They kept their noses in books all the time.

One time, I was absent and missed a test in my English class in literature. I went to visit my college professor, who had a PhD in literature. He was a bachelor, of about fifty, and had never been married. I went to see him to see if I could make up the exam that I missed. It was at night, and do you know what I found that that joker was doing? He was reading Shakespeare! He got his jollies by reading literature. Literature was his life!

He had shelves, in his classroom, from one end of the room to the other end, from floor to ceiling, with hundreds of books on literature and poetry. And I'm telling you, this professor could quote every sentence in each of those books. I remember, many times, that he would quote a verse or a sentence from a book and then ask a student to go to the book shelves to row so and so, to book number so and so, and read sentence so and so of page so and so and it would be verbatim per the professor's quote (and the professor would gleefully jump up and down, and get his jollies, when the student read what he had quoted).

An egghead, that's what he was. And I found that most of my college professors, with PhD's, were like that.

And it seems to me (Lord, I hope I'm wrong) that most of our high school teachers, today, are getting to be like those college professors. It doesn't seem that teachers, today, try to be the best teachers that they can possibly be (I think they are more interested in how much money they can make). They form unions (up North. I don't think they have In the South....yet) to put pressure on state and local governments to give them a raise in every budget. Money is their primary concern (along with wanting to be recognized as ed-u-ca-tors).

Teachers, in my boyhood years were just ducky.

# CLICHÉ NO. 66

## HOOK, LINE, AND SINKER

It's best not to lie. It's best to tell the truth at all times. If you always tell the truth, you don't have to worry when someone asks you about something that happened years ago. You will probably give the same answer that you did back then. But, if you lied back then, the chances are you will not remember all the details of your lie, and you will give a different answer, and they will catch you in a bald face lie, and they will never, ever trust you again. Ain't that terrible? That's bad!

It's best not to lie, even if the truth hurts. Keep your conscience clear, and sharp, and clean (that way you won't have to rack your brains and maybe get all sweaty and nervous, and agitated trying to make up something to lie your way out of a bad situation).

But, if you feel the truth will hurt you too much, or if you feel that the truth will hurt someone you love, and you cannot bear to tell the truth, make sure that the lies you tell are little bitty white

212

lies. Don't tell whoppers. People will believe little white lies a whole lot quicker that they will believe whoppers.

Most fishermen lie. That's part of the joy they get from fishing. And I can understand why fishermen lie. Can't you? It's no fun going fishing and sitting on the bank, or in a boat out in the water, with the blazing sun beating down on you, and the gnats swarming all around you, and not get a bite all day. That's not fun!

And a lot of fishermen do just that (not get a bite all day). The truth would hurt them so bad (and might hurt their innocent little boys, who think their dads are supermen). So, the fishermen make up a story about the big fish (a big, big fish. A 10 pound blue gill), that broke the 100 pound test line, and got away!

That's a little white lie, and it won't hurt anyone ,except the fisherman, and if he doesn't stop telling tales like that, he might start believing them himself, and he might get such joy that his tales will get bigger and bigger until he starts telling whoppers, and people will stop believing anything he says.

For example, look at the tale that a fisherman out in Pascagula, Mississippi told. He was fishing, when a UFO landed on the stream and aliens zapped him with a ray gun, and took him aboard their craft and put him through brain scans, organ scans, and then put him back in his boat and then the UFO sailed away.

Who, in their right mind, would believe a tale like that? Nobody, not even another fisherman!

And look at another example: A certain politician, a presidential candidate, said, with his chest poked out: "I invented the internet." Who, in their right mind, would believe a tale like that? Nobody, except maybe other politicians who tell whoppers that are bigger than that!

I bet that fisherman from Mississippi and that presidential candidate wish, now, that they had never told those whoppers. Whoppers will follow you all the days of your life. Little white lies won't hurt all that bad.

You hear the voice of experience talking. You better listen to me. I know what I'm talking about. I have told a few white lies in my life (only a few), and I told one big whopper. The little white lies don't bother me, but Lord, I wish I had never told that whopper!

Let me tell you about the whopper: I found an extra key, in mama's coat hanging on a door in the kitchen, a key to mama's 1936 ford car (with a rumble seat). I took that key and put it in my pocket. I used another key, a key on mama's key ring, to drive mama to work in Jackson's mill. I was sixteen. After I parked the car, under a shade tree, and after mama had gone into the mill to work (she took the key that was on the key ring with her), I was supposed to mess around town, with my buddies (for eight hours), until she got off work, then, I would drive her home. But that night, I didn't mess around town with my buddies. I had a spare key to the car. So, I used it and picked up some of my buddies and we went gallivanting all over town and outa town!

I used mama's precious gas (not all of it) that she had worked her fingers to the bone to purchase. What a low down rotten scoundrel I was, and I admit it!

On the way home that night, I guess mama had looked at the gas gauge and saw that the car didn't have as much gas as she thought it should have, she began to look very suspicious at me (like she knew that I had found that spare key in her coat pocket). She didn't say anything. She didn't ask me if I had found the key. But, when we got home and got out of the car, she tried to beat me into the house.

I beat her, but she was right behind me, and I didn't have time to go to her coat hanging on the door and put that key back in her coat pocket. So, I just slightly, underhand, pitched that key, aiming at her coat pocket. And lo and behold, I didn't hear the key hit the floor, so I thought that it must have went into the pocket (but I was not sure).

I turned and went to the kitchen sink and pretended that I was thirsty, that's the reason I was in such a hurry to get in the house, and I got myself a glass of water.

Mama saw that I didn't go near her coat, but she didn't see my underhand pitch, and she rushed over to her coat. I was as nervous as an old setting hen when she ran her hand into the coat pocket.

When she came out with the key, a happy smile came over her face. She came over to me and gave me a kiss on my cheek.

She was sorry that she had not trusted her son (Her lying, good for nothing, low down, rotten, son! Lord, I wish I could tell mama the truth, now, but it's too late)!

She fell for my big whopper of a lie "hook, line, and sinker"

That big lie will go with me to my grave. I'm sorry. I'm sorry. Hey! Did you hear me? I'm sorry.

If you are going to lie, tell little white lies. Whoppers hurt too bad!

# CLICHÉ NO. 67

## UP THE CREEK WITHOUT A PADDLE

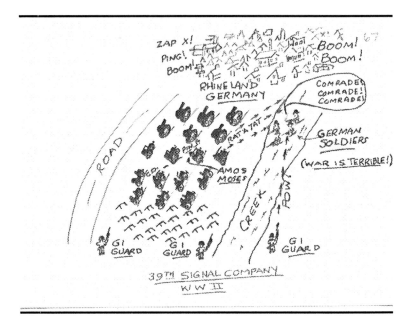

War is no fun. It's no fun for the GIs. It's no fun for the enemy. It's no fun for civilians. Maybe, one day, we will learn this and start loving everybody, even our enemies.

I volunteered for the army during World War II. I was brave and patriotic and eager to go fight the Axis (I also knew that Uncle Sam would draft me anyway. So, I volunteered to get a better deal).

The army sent me to school and I became a radio repair technician and later a telephone linesman.

I had a gun, a forty five caliber submachine gun that looked similar to a grease gun, but I never did shoot anybody (except, one time, I almost shot myself in the foot, accidentally).

Nobody ever shot at me either, except my company commander almost shot me, accidentally, one night, when we were camped outside a town named Rhineland, Germany (our signal company was camped), while our infantry was trying to clean out the town. Small arms fire and big guns, too, were lighting up the sky. My sergeant (I was a corporal) put me on guard duty with a fifty caliber machine gun, which was a big gun mounted in a half track vehicle. I had never shot a gun like that in my life. He showed me how to shoot it, and I was to stand guard from midnight until two am.

The place, where we were located, was about a mile from the town where all the action was taking place. We were camped in a grass field between a roadway and a small creek. The creek had bushes on each side. Guards, with rifles, were posted on each side of the creek and up at the road. I and the other GIs with machine guns were instructed to open fire and spray the creek and road with bullets, if we heard the guards shoot.

Well, shortly before I was to go off guard duty at two am, and let another GI take over the machine gun, one of the guards by the creek heard some Germans coming up the creek and he shot! Immediately, machine guns, all around me, started shooting! Rat-a-tat-tat! I said to my comrades, who were bunkered down in the half track: "Boys we are being attacked! I pulled on the handle of my machine gun and tried to get a bullet in the chamber, so I could do some shooting, too. But, something was wrong with the gun. It was jammed. The bullet wouldn't go in the chamber. And luckily, too, I guess, for there ain't no telling who I would have shot. Those big guns are hard to handle. I just might have sprayed my own troops.

The Germans began to cry out: "Comrade, Comrade!" Our company commander shouted: "Hold your fire!"

Four or five Germans were trying to escape from the town by going up the creek. One or two had been shot and wounded very badly (I told you war is no fun). Our medics got them out and started treating their wounds.

That's what you call: "Up the creek without a paddle!" The poor Germans, I felt sorry for them. They were only trying to quit fighting and go back to their homes.

Well, no sooner had our medics rescued the wounded Germans, and things had settled down and gotten quiet again (except for the big guns going off in town), when BANG! A bullet whizzed past my ear. I could feel the breeze from it! I hollered: "Who, in the hell, fired that shot!" A voice from the darkness said: "I did, and I'm sorry. My gun went off!" It was, none other than, my company commander. The stupid jerk almost shot me. If he had, then I wouldn't be here to tell you "war is no fun"!

# CLICHÉ NO. 68

## JACKS OF ALL TRADES

Hard work, and rough times, and tribulations build character (The type of character that is self confident, strong willed, and self reliant). That's why America is strong. America's foundation was the pilgrims, settlers, pioneers, frontiersmen, farmers, hunters and trappers. These people who had to eke out a living through many hardships, hostilities, trials, and tribulations. They were, truly, jacks of all trades!

And another thing: Everyone knows that the backbone of families, neighborhoods, churches, towns, and cities is the mamas!

It's mama who has to be the doctor. It's mama who has to make the home with all the doo dads and trinkets, flower pots, pictures, etc.. It's mama who has to do the cooking, and washing, and ironing, and cleaning house. It's mama who has to be the emotional one and kiss boo boos, wipe away tears, and hug their babies and rock them to sleep.

What would the world do without our mamas?? America's pioneer mamas were the best mamas in the world.

The pioneer men had it tough doing things like: blazing trails through the wilderness, during all kinds of weather, and hunting and trapping animals, killing snakes, and Indians, too, sometimes; but, the pioneer women had it even tougher!

They had to stay home alone for weeks at a time, while their husbands were on their expeditions, and don't you know that those pioneer women got lonely, and worried, and scared for their safety and for their husbands' safety, and for the safety of their little ones??

It was so bad that some of the pioneer women died at an early age due to "cabin fever" (in case you don't know it, cabin fever is grieving oneself to death).

When we talk about a woman's work is never done, I'm sure we are talking about a pioneer woman's work, and not a modern woman who spends most of her time shopping and watching TV.

I, sometimes, brag that I'm a jack of all trades because I can do a little bit of carpentry, electrical, and plumbing works; but I tell you frankly, women have got me beat all to pieces. I could never do all the things that women do. I don't know how, and I don't have the patience. For example: One time, I took some dirty clothes to a Laundromat. I put the clothes in the washer and added, what I thought, was the right amount of soap powder. When the washer started, soapsuds began to come out of the washer, flooded the Laundromat with soapsuds, and went out the door and down the street! I ain't washed another load of clothes since.

In the early days of America, pioneer women and women down South and out West had to know how to cook, sew, tan leather, shoot a muzzle loader, cut firewood, make lye soap, be a doctor to their children, and deliver babies for their neighbors.

America owes a lot to our forefathers and even more to our foremamas. They were jacks of all trades.

# CLICHÉ NO. 69

## THAT'S THE LAST STRAW

THATCHED ROOF IN IRELAND

STRAW

STRAW TIC MATRESS

Straw played an important role in the lives of people, in years gone by, especially down South and in Ireland. However, its usage has faded. Today, straw is used mainly for covering freshly seeded lawns, shoulders of roads, and for decorations at Halloween time. But, I think that the Irish may still use straw to make thatch roofs for their picturesque little white stucco houses. I've seen some of them. They are unique. I don't know what kind of straw they use for the thatched roofs, but I'm sure that it is not oat straw. Oat straw doesn't last long. That's the reason we use it to cover freshly seeded areas for grass. Oat straw, and wheat straw, too, rots fast.

We don't grow nearly as much oats and wheat, down South, as we used to grow. That's another reason why we don't have as many usages for straw. The South has just about quit farming and gone to making automobiles, computers, digital cameras, and cell phones (and buying them, too).

The South is not what it used to be. (You Yankees better quit making fun of us and start taking us serious). The South is on the move. Before you know it, we will over take you Yankees, and, yes, pass you in our BMWs. Toyotas, and Mercedes (cars built down South), and you will be caught with your britches down, and you will stand in awe of us, and you will wake up and get those foolish ideas out of your heads (ideas about the South being unlearned and ignorant), and you will want to move down South (away from the ice cycles and snow banks). Many Yankees have already moved here (the smart ones).

But, in years gone by, the South deserved the bad opinions that the Yankees had of us. We were unlearned (the vast majority of Southerners). We were farmers, and farmers didn't need very much education and technical training (that's what the old timers thought). The South was a land of straw hats, straw tick mattresses, straw bedding for our mules and cows, straw mats for our front doors, piles of straw for kids to play in (maybe, if you are an old Southerner, you can help me out and add some uses that we made of straw). The South had so much straw that we couldn't give it away (Now days you have to pay five dollars for a bale).

Have you ever slept on a straw mattress? I haven't either but some Southerners did. They called the mattresses "straw ticks". The mattress cover was a thick, stripped cloth that had an opening through which straw was stuffed. Some Southerners, the dirt poor ones, used corn shucks instead of straw. The straw, and corn shucks, wouldn't last long, maybe just a few months, and had to be changed for fresh straw and shucks. When I was a lad, folks had just about quit using straw ticks and had started using factory made mattresses stuffed with cotton. The cotton mattresses were solid with buttons about every six inches.

But some beds had feather mattresses. That's the kind that I slept on. When we killed a chicken (almost every Sunday), mama saved the feathers to use to stuff mattresses and pillows. The feather beds were very soft and snug and comfortable. Many, many times mama had to threaten me, with a stick, before I would get out of that bed! Then, World War II came along and I had to leave my feather bed. I joined the army and went off to war. At Camp Crowder, Missouri, where I took my basic training, we had bunk beds with cotton mattresses. We had bunk beds, with cotton mattresses, at the radio repair technical school and at the Aviation

Cadets' training school (Springfield College) that I attended. But, after I finished my training, I was shipped to the European Theater of Operations and the beds that I slept on over there were a horse of a different color.

Sometimes, those beds were no beds at all. They were sacks: a sleeping bag on the ground, or a sleeping bag on concrete, or a sleeping bag in a pile of straw (that was a pretty good bed that I had in Pont-A-Mousan, France). But, back then, I could sleep anywhere, in any kind of bed, because I was young and in good physical condition.

But, for several years now, I have been sleeping in beds with extra firm inner spring mattresses and with box springs. My bones are old and my muscles get cramps and it would kill me (it would be the last straw), if I had to give up my bed and sleep in a different type bed!

"Straw tick mattresses"?? Man, I'm glad we don't have to sleep on them anymore! How about you??

# CLICHÉ NO. 70

## OUT OF THE WAY PLACES

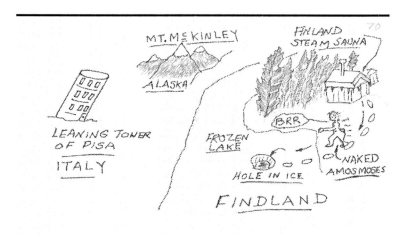

I never dreamed, when I was a little ole barefooted country boy, that the Good Lord would take me to so many beautiful, faraway places around the world.

I know that there are a lot of rich folks: lawyers, doctors, politicians, evangelists, etc., that have traveled to more places than I have, but I guarantee that there are very, very few poor ole Southern farm boys (who picked cotton, and plowed a mule) that have seen more of the world than me. I have flat been around! And I give thanks to my Good Lord! I don't know why he took me to so many places. I haven't quite figured it out, but I know that He has a purpose and I will understand it all by and by.

It would just blow your mind, like it has mine, to know how poor my family was (dirt poor. I'm talking about sho 'nough dirt poor). My "paw" was a cotton farmer, down South. That's about as poor as one can get. My "maw" worked in a cotton mill (lint heads were what cotton mill workers were called).

No one in my family of ten kids had ever finished high school until I came along (I'm third from youngest). I'm not bragging.

224

I'm complaining. I'm complaining that I had to be the one to blaze the way. I'm complaining that I had no one in my family who had been there that I could go to and pick their brains for some guidance.

But what will really, really blow your mind (like it has mine) is how the Lord picked me out of all the others in my dirt poor Southern family and sent me to college, paid my tuition, fed me, clothed me, and gave me a car to drive.

But what will really, really, really, blow your mind (like it has mine) is how the Lord, not only sent me to college but He sent me to the best college in the whole world: "Clemson College". GO TIGERS!! FIGHT!! FIGHT!! FIGHT!!

But what will really, really, really, really blow your mind (like it has mine) is how the Lord gave this poor ole dirt poor Southern boy (who picked cotton and plowed a mule) enough sense and brains to study and persevere and graduate in a very, very hard course, electrical engineering I don't see how I done it. (All those electrons are enough to blow anyone's mind).

But what will really, really, really, really, really, blow your mind (like it has mine) is how the Lord gave me the experience and know how to pass the state board examinations and to become a registered professional engineer in several states (That blows the mind of this ole Southern boy who picked cotton and plowed a mule).

Through my profession I got to see the world. Some of the places that the Lord has taken me: England, Scotland, Ireland, France, Luxemburg, Holland, Belgium, Finland, Denmark, Sweden, Norway, Italy, Austria, Switzerland, Germany, Czechoslovakia, Puerto Rica, St. Thomas, St Croix, Mexico, Panama, Peru, Japan, Taiwan, Singapore, Malaysia, Canada, Newfoundland, Alaska, and all over the USA from coast to coast and from north to south (in addition, the lord has allowed me to fly over and view many other beautiful places from the air, places that He created by His own hands).

I reminisce, sometimes, about all the beautiful, out of the way places in the world that I have visited. Places like: No. 1. The snow capped mountain, Mt. McKinley in Alaska, and also the moose, and polar bears, and glaciers. No. 2. The Orangutan sanctuary in the Jungles of Malaysia. It was feeding time. We ran out into the jungles to watch Orangutans, with babies clinging to their backs, swinging on the vines through the tall thick trees, coming to get bananas that the Malaysian sanctuary attendants brought for the apes. No. 3. The Tower of London and Big Ben. The London zoo where I saw my first hippopotamus up close. The centuries old Canterbury Cathedral. No. 4. The Inca Indians ruins in Cuzco, Peru, the llamas, and the mummy of the Spanish conqueror (I forgot his name) on display in Lima. No. 5. The white birch forests of Finland containing huge granite boulders throughout the forests (blows ones mind how those boulders got there), and I will never forget the cabin, located alone out in the wilderness, on an ice covered lake. My host, an executive of an airport lighting equipment manufacturing company of Finland took us there. He cooked our dinner, himself, and served some kind of seafood like I had never tasted before: A big round ball, about eight inches in diameter, of crusty baked bread. Inside the ball was a mixture of vegetables and seafood (maybe you have seen it and tasted it. It was yummy delicious). After dinner, we went to a hut in the forest where there was an original Finish steam sauna bath. We stripped off naked, and our host poured water over red-hot coals in the sauna and steam boiled. We sat on benches and sweat and sweat. Then, we ran from the hut, naked and as fast as we could run, for it was cold, and jumped through a hole in the ice into the cold lake. Wow! Talking about a shock!

But after we went back to the hut and dried off and put our clothes back on, we felt good, like walking on cloud nine! No. 6. The canals of Holland and Norway. There are some rich folks that live in Norway in picturesque mansions on the banks of canals. Their houses looked like castles to this ole country boy who was raised in a country shack. No. 7. A Vikings' museum in Stockholm, Sweden. There was a skull of a Viking that had been killed in a sword fight. The skull had a crack in it of about six inches. Beside the skull was the Viking's armored helmet, with a hinged face. The helmet had the same cut through the top. The fight happened eons ago (So long ago that it blows one's mind. At least, it did mine). No. 8. A ski lift ride up in the Alps of Austria (what a fantastic view). At the top there was a mountaineer's simple home and a small barn, and big white and brown cows and all had cow-bells. I don't see what kept the cows from falling over the cliffs. There were no fences. When I was there, the mountaineer was trying to push a contrary calf into the barn. The calf didn't want to go. It wanted to stay outside with her mama. I know that the mountaineer must have gotten lonely, way up there all by himself, when tourist season was over (blows my mind).

I could go on and on (the Leaning Tower of Pisa. The castles of Scotland and Germany (Old, old. I'm talking about sho 'nough old). Churches on the sides of mountains throughout Europe.

I know that I'm boring you to death so I'll stop.

The Lord has made a beautiful world, and what's so great is He took me by my hand and showed me all those beautiful out of the way places. (Such rare, old, antiques, beautiful, picturesque places).

But what really blows my mind is why the Lord would be mindful of me, a nobody, a son of a dirt poor Southern farmer, certainly a run of the mill type fellow as far as the world is concerned. Why in the world would the Lord select me, of all people? I think I know. He did it for me because He loves me. I know He loves me. This I know for the Bible tells me so. That's the reason!

I don't deserve it. None of us do. If I got what I deserved, I would still be plowing a mule, in some out of the way place, out in the sticks, like my "paw", and I wouldn't know beans about what the rest of the world looks like.

The Lord is so good. He's so good to me!

Thank you for reading my book. I hope you enjoyed it.

Amos Moses Terry

# About The Author

Amos Moses Terry is a son of a poor dirt farmer of the South. He was a young lad during the great depression. His mother labored in a cotton mill to help support the family.

He is a graduate of Clemson University, with a degree in electrical engineering. He has been licensed in several states to practice professional engineering. He is retired from the Federal Aviation Administration. He was the FAA Southern Region's Airport Lighting Engineer. While with them, he was the author of several books and technical drawings that were distributed to the aviation community, world wide, at the Paris air show.

Since his retirement, he has spent his time remodeling an old colonial home, cruising around town in his sports convertible, and writing his memoirs. This book, "Cliches And Common Sense", is his second book. The first was "Horse Sense and Birdhouses".

Amos Moses Terry has suffered some hard times, like a lot of other hard working Southerners, but he has come up out of the dirt and is proud to tell you that he is from Dixie, a way down South in Dixie. (But he is, in no way, biased. He loves all people of the world, red and yellow, black and white, even Yankees).

Be happy and have a nice day.

Printed in the United States
34444LVS00006B/1-63